SYLVAN BEACH, NEW YORK

- On The Lake Oneida -

A HISTORY

or

Tales of the Vienna Woods

by

JACK HENKE

NORTH COUNTRY BOOKS

Box 506 — Sylvan Beach, N. Y. 13157

First Printing—January, 1975

Revised Edition — June, 1980

ISBN 978-1-4930-7672-7

PRINTING BY BOONVILLE GRAPHICS, INC., BOONVILLE, N. Y.

. . . At last you emerge into the country of Oneida and Lewis Counties — it was misty, just at sundown, and beautiful, the mist lying along the green silky fields, the blurred orange light in the sky (the next day, clear, liquid and bright — white yellow, and orange) — it always gives rise in me up here to a kind of lofty and purified thoughts: dignity and beauty of the country which somehow has enobled the lives of the people and all that old story of their immigration and their living, away from New England, among the hills and the fields and the forests, where they were all alone, but independent — free, flourishing — their human relationships and labors against the non-human grandeur of the setting — riding along those up and down hills, a man behind a horse in a buggy, a farm wagon or carriage, under the high heavens, with fluid orange light or dark blue thunder clouds.

— EDMUND WILSON
Upstate, June 16-18, 1950

The music lives — Sylvan Beach, Oneida Lake

Preface

Sylvan Beach is a small, recently incorporated village in upstate New York. The village sinews for about a mile along the eastern shores of the Lake Oneida, largest of New York's inland waters. Lake Oneida has roughly twenty-two miles east-west and an average of four miles north-south. It is a powerful lake, commanding both the serene pastoral and the relentless amoral tempest scenes. On the far eastern shores of the lake were five miles of immaculate sand beach, forming a pure corridor between the lake and a deep deciduous forest. The beach explains east shore placenames, "Sylvan Beach," "Verona Beach" and "Oakland Beach," the latter being now defunct. Beach and lake made these islands of upstate civilization possible. They are resorts, vacation spas for the upstate New Yorker.

Sylvan Beach, New York — A History or *Tales of the Vienna Woods* is the story of one upstate village from its birth in the Lake Oneida country to the present day. Like many upstate communities, the village's history has been fashioned by the panoramic countryside in which it is nestled. There is much space in upstate New York, space that allows man to be placed in a proper, proportioned diminutive, living off his country's resources yet not controlling or dominating the landscape. He makes use of what he has and, even where his civilization forms large cities, there is a still larger force, that which Wilson called the "non-human grandeur of the setting," to which he can turn for reflection of his origin and history as well as for rest and repose. Understanding this "larger force," the upstate country, and man's development through it is the key to knowing upstate history. Wilson worked with the idea in words, the artists of the Hudson River school of painting used oil-paint and canvas. My medium is history.

History cannot be a totally written thing. We can observe it in the photograph, find its color in the painting, interpret its spirit in architecture, in individual persons themselves. Take a drive down the Mohawk Valley, walk Albany's State Street, fish for sturgeon at Verplank-on-Hudson, live with the ideas and words of a cogent observer of the past and see, hear, feel history around you. It can be a satisfying feeling and a stimulating one. It can make you want to know more. I met Sylvan Beach that way.

The subtitle, *Tales of the Vienna Woods,* is dedicated to the spirit of this book. It arose in animated conversation with friends during my first weeks of research. Sylvan Beach is in Vienna township; Sylvan derives meaning from the Latin "sylvanus," or "wooded." Thus the "Vienna Woods," with great debt to Strauss for his "Tales," found this history zealot's fancy. It was a happy title then, as happy and eager as I was, engulfed in a discovery and creation that would last two and one-half years. It makes good sense to use it now.

Table of Contents

To LLOYD BLANKMAN
An upstate New Yorker who loved his country

A MAP ORIENTATION TO THE SYLVAN BEACH AREA

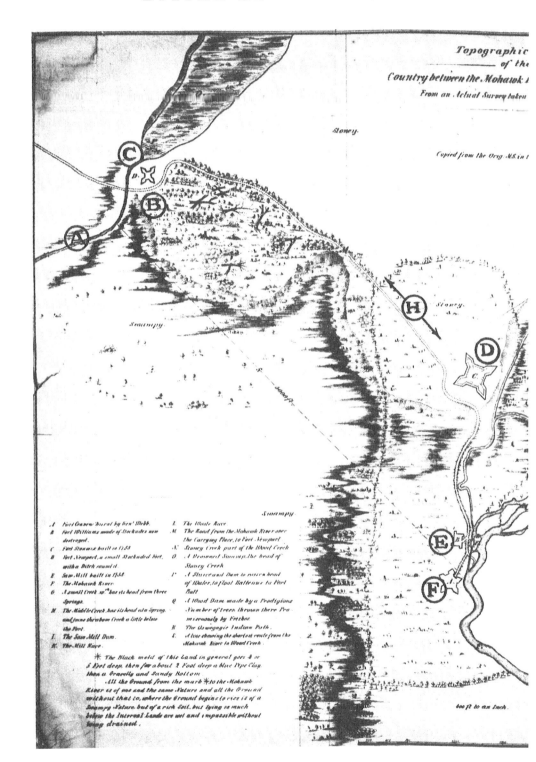

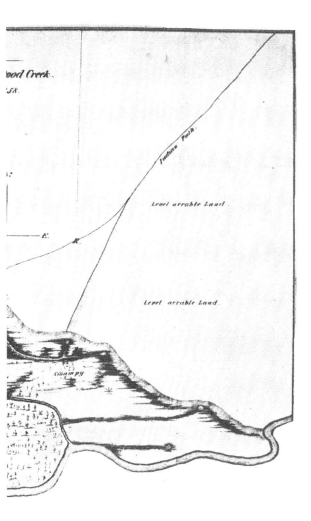

— THE "ONEIDA CARRY," 1758 —

This is a colonial map of The Carry region, between the Mohawk River and Wood Creek. For details, follow this letter key.

A. Wood Creek
B. Fort Newport, built near
C. A sluiceway, used to swell the creek's volume during summer drought.

D. Fort Stanwix
E. Fort Williams, a crude stockade
F. Fort Craven
G. The Mohawk River
H. The "Carry" Route

These forts were British protection for The Carry from French attacks. Fort Bull was to the west (left) of this map's area.

(Map I and II courtesy Oneida County Historical Association)

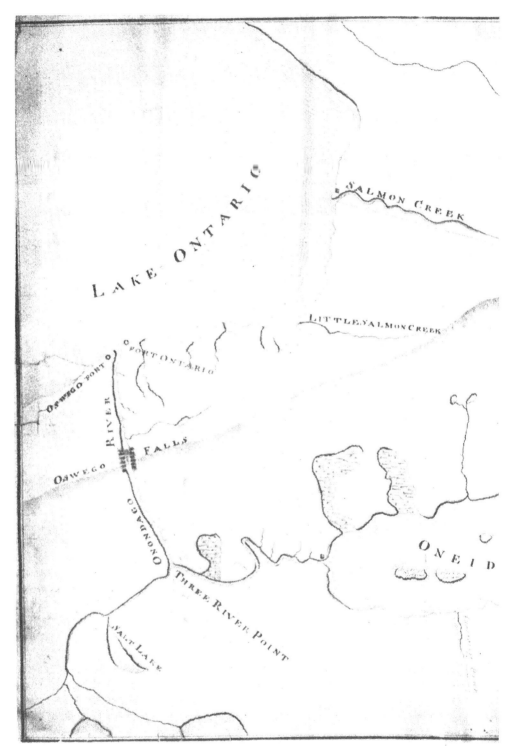

— LAKE ONEIDA REGION, 1780 —

This map, while showing several inaccuracies, is useful in documenting the colonial trade and transportation route through Oneida Lake. All is well-labeled, except the Mohawk River, which journeys eastward from Fort Stan-

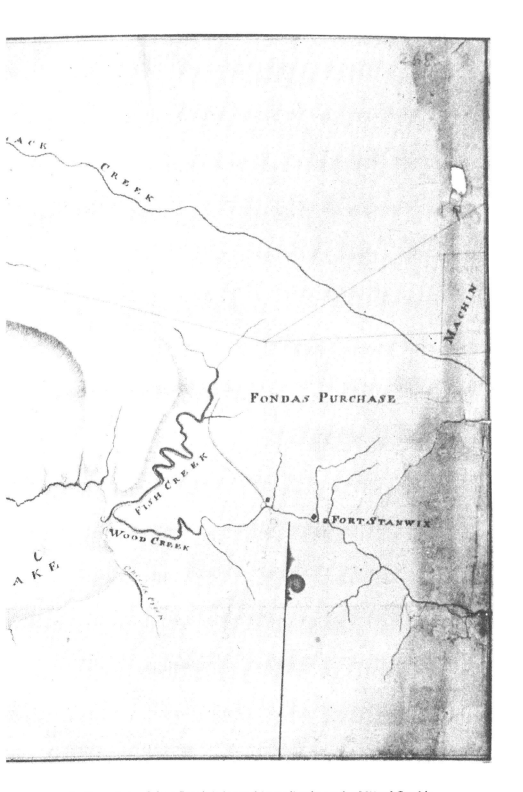

wix. Present-day Sylvan Beach is located immediately north of Wood Creek's mouth, on Oneida's eastern shore. The city of Rome rises today at the Fort Stanwix site. Despite its twisted nature, this route was very convenient for colonials.

SYLVAN BEACH

Scale in Feet

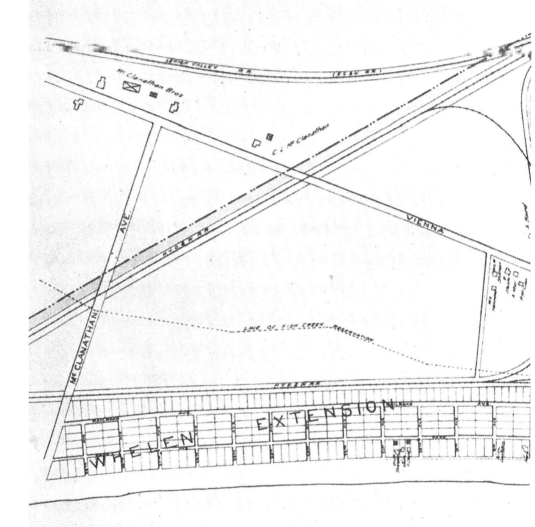

O N E I D A

— SYLVAN BEACH, 1907 —

This is Sylvan Beach in the heart of its "Cavana Era," prior to the Barge Canal's construction. On the right (south) of the map is the canal's planned course, cutting across Wood River's meanders. Two piers jut into the lake. The left (northern) pier was The Saint Charles' dock, directly west from the hotel. The other was associated with Cavana's Sanitarium, east of the pier. The Municipal Park is bordered by Railroad Avenue (east) and Park Avenue

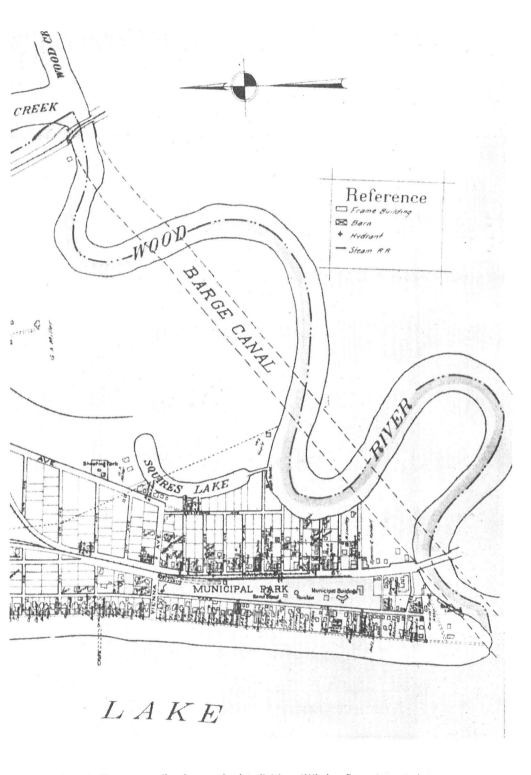

Reference

☐ Frame Building
☒ Barn
♦ Hydrant
— Steam R.R

WOOD CR

CREEK

WOOD

BARGE CANAL

RIVER

SQUIRES LAKE

MUNICIPAL PARK

LAKE

(west). One can easily observe the lot division (Whelen Extension, etc.) that accommodated the village's expansion. The village is thoroughly settled today, with homes and vacation cottages filling the area from the canal line to McClanathan Avenue (named for the former family bearing that name). Squires Lake (now called National Lake) is an oxbow lake, formed by Wood River's meandering.

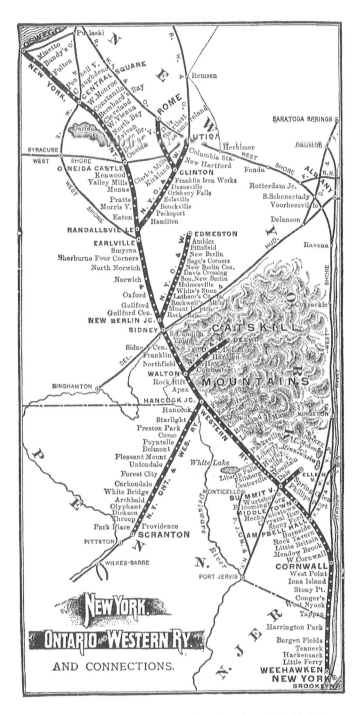

O & W Railroad map, showing Sylvan Beach and Oneida Lake
north shore stations, around 1900.

LAKE ONEIDA, THE EARLY YEARS

Sylvan Beach is a picturesque spot with its shady groves and, in addition to what nature has done for it, has a history that makes comment about it always interesting.

— from a local paper, 1899

In the beginning there were the Iroquois. They hunted upstate's woods, farmed its fields, fished its rivers and lakes long before the white man arrived. The Iroquois were a civilized people. They lived in villages, self-contained units, dependent on no outsider, no thruway or railroad. They organized a confederacy, a mutual defense pact among their five tribes, the "Five Nations." The white man vied for alliance with the confederacy and the Iroquois toyed with loyalties, skillfully dealing with the people that would, in time, destroy them.

The Iroquois lived Lake Oneida. The western end of the lake was Onondaga country. In the east were the Oneidas, the people with whom we shall be most concerned. The Oneidas, a people of distinct culture and language, were frequent visitors to the Sylvan Beach area. They came there to fish and, to a lesser degree, to farm. Their central villages were located south of the Beach, near present-day Munnsville and Oneida Castle, the latter named for an Indian fortress, the "Castle." The Oneida villages were always near water, a dependable source of food and transportation.

The Oneida's language flowed with music of their country. The words, their structure, were staffs of vowels weaving consonants in the pattern of their land. There was no Oneida Lake, there was Ga-no-a-lo-hale. There was O-na-yote-ga-o-no-go, land of the Oneidas. Te-on-na-tale was the "pine forest." Wood Creek, Ka-no-go-dick. Fish Creek, Ta-ga-soke, "forked like a spear."[1] Say these words and feel their rhythm. Let their symphony take you with them, to their departed country.

The Oneidas fished Ta-ga-soke, the Fish Creek. They fished to eat and they fished with ceremony. An elaborate fishing rite governed spring fishing. It was spring when the salmon returned to Oneida and, in Ta-ga-soke and other tributaries, they spawned. The salmon lived in the Indians' waters from May to December and the Oneidas fished for them, beginning their harvest with an annual spring rite.

A prominent 18th century Oneida chieftain was Ske-nandoa. The man received eulogy on a stone in the Hamilton College graveyard. The stone reads:

> . . . Wise, eloquent, and brave, he long swayed the councils of his tribe, whose confidence and affection he eminently enjoyed. In the war which placed the Canadas under the crown of Great Britain he was actively engaged against the French: in that of the revolution, he espoused that of the colonies and ever afterward remained a firm friend to the United States. Under the ministry of the Rev. Mr. Kirkland he embraced the doctrines of the gospel, and having exhibited their power in a long life adorned by every Christian virtue, he fell asleep in Jesus at the advanced age of one hundred years.

Skenandoa undoubtedly participated and probably directed fishing operations on the Ta-ga-soke. Once, let us postulate, he sent a message to all sachem of the Oneidas. The directive might have read:

> My brothers: Great heaven blesses us with the return of our salmon to Ga-no-a-lo-hale. Messengers tell me that the Ta-ga-soke virtually teems with the silver fishes. Now, as is the custom and the necessity, we must begin our fishing. One member of each family must go to the stream by

three days time to celebrate the Great Spirit's goodness to his people. Tarry not, brethren, for you know winter's food depends on spring's harvest. Creatures of the wild must not reject its bounty.

One member of each Oneida family came to Ta-ga-soke.

They came. The men drove stakes across the stream's mouth. They filled the openings between each stake with brush gathered by women and children, thus forming an effective barrier to any fish. Salmon were driven toward this weir and, when they were close to it, another brush-stake net was built upstream. The Oneidas had trapped their fish.

Warriors entered the stream, armed with spears, knives and clubs. They slashed at the salmon, killing or wounding many with each thrust. Downstream, their families collected dead and wounded salmon as they floated past. After several hours, when all salmon were harvested, a feast occurred, a feast deemed "the piscatorial picnic of the Oneidas" by one Sylvan Beach historian.[2] For the Oneidas, it was a way of life.

The salmon came to Oneida. "Came" is the word. The construction of dams in the Oswego River and, basically, the spread of the white mans' civilization to Upstate brought on the salmon's extinction. By the late 19th century, all were gone. The river dams stopped salmon migration. They could not pass through these stone barriers. The salmon live today in names, "Salmon River" and "Salmon Creek," both feeders of Ontario. They live in memory, in some men's dreams to bring them back, in words of the historian.

The white man came. The salmon run and Iroquois civilization are now dreams and empty phrases.

Folklore abounds on the subject of the Oneida Indians. Mostly "lore" and less "folk," the stories provide insight into a white man's attitude toward the Indian. For many whites the Indian was a sort of mystical being with strange rituals and untapped riches. The latter unknown created an aura of strangeness about the Indian. Where did the Indian bury his gold and silver? That question plagued Lake Oneida area settlers in the 1800's. It gave rise to this folk tale, the "Lost Treasure of the Oneidas.[3]

*   *   *   *   *

On the northern shore of Oneida Lake, about thirteen miles west of the City of Rome, there is a forgotten cemetery of the Oneida Indians. Old timers living in the vicinity swear that a great treasure lies buried there in a grave, guarded by the spirit of an Oneida Chief.

At various intervals throughout the year a ball of fire, resembling an orange in shape, hovers in the air twenty feet above the treasure trove. For over a century countless treasure hunters have vainly tried to discover the source of the mysterious light and locate the buried hoard, but when they reach a certain point near the sacred Oneida ground, the light vanishes, to reappear mockingly as the seekers turn back.

Long before most of the Oneida moved to Green Bay, Wisconsin (1823), a family named Belknap owned a tract of land adjacent to the northern boundary of the reservation.

One night the elder Belknap had a dream. In his dream an Oneida warrior appeared before him. He motioned for the farmer to follow him. Belknap walked with him through the cleared fields of his land and the woods beyond. At length they came to the old Indian cemetery. The Indian then took Belknap by the arm and led him to a certain spot in the sacred ground.

"Here lies a great Chief of the Oneidas'," the warrior

said in the language of his people. Belknap, who had no knowledge of the Oneida tongue, was amazed to discover he understood every word.

"Here lies, buried with him, a stone crock containing the treasure of the Oneidas, the gold and silver taken from the French and the gold and jewels of the Spaniards who once settled on our land. The Gods of my fathers have given you this treasure. Go and bring tools to dig. When you find the stone crock containing this treasure, you must turn around three times before you try to remove it. If you do not do this simple thing, the Gods will be angered and the treasure will be lost from all men forever. Hear me, my brother. I have spoken."

The warrior was then silent. There was a rumble of thunder in the sky, and Belknap found himself standing alone in the cemetery. It was then he awakened from his dream. He gathered his tools and finally came to the cemetery and experienced no difficulty in locating the exact spot that his warrior guide had pointed out.

Belknap set to work furiously with his tools. In a short time his pick struck a piece of flagstone, breaking it in half. There, before his eyes, was the stone crock with the jewels and gold reflecting the light of the morning sun.

The farmer cried out in excitement. He forgot the instructions to turn around three times before touching the treasure. He tossed aside his tools and fell to his knees, greedily tearing away the dirt surrounding the crock with his bare hands. The treasure stood free at last.

There was a rumble of distant thunder in the cloudless sky, but Belknap failed to hear it. He laid eager fingers on the rim of the crock. The earth seemed then to tremble as a bolt of lightning flashed downward. Belknap threw up his hands and sprawled headlong beside the crock he had uncovered.

It was dusk when the farmer regained consciousness and was able to crawl to his home. He was put to bed and remained there for several days, suffering from shock. When he had recovered sufficiently, he hurried to the cemetery. He found the excavation he had made, but there was no sign of the crock containing the treasure or any indication that there had been one in the Indian grave.

That night the ball of fire appeared for the first time, swaying over the spot where the treasure had been.

It has been said that Belknap spent the rest of his life trying to find the lost treasure. The Gods had chosen him to share the riches of the Oneidas, but he had allowed greed to betray their trust.

Other stories exist that attribute "sacred ground" or "sacred stones" around Lake Oneida to the Oneida Indians. Most likely, all these sagas are false; inconsistencies, exemplified by the statement of Spanish settlements that existed on Oneida land in the "Belknap fiasco," cast doubt on the stories' authenticity. These tales authors never found their crocks filled with Indian gold and silver, but their imaginations certainly overflowed.

The first white man, so history tells me, to visit Lake Oneida was the French explorer-soldier Samuel de Champlain. Samuel became no friend to the Iroquois. He took the side of their enemy, the Algonquin, and fought the Confederacy's forces many times. These activities of the warlike Champlain were to reverberate through history as they, historians conjecture, were a possible cause for the Iroquois-English alliance in the French and Indian Wars.

Champlain's diary of 1615 contained reference to the Ontario-Oneida region.[4]

All canoes being thus concealed, we left the

bank of the lake, which is 80 leagues long and 25
wide (Lake Ontario). It is inhabited for the
greater part by Savages, along the sides of the
streams, and we continued our course by land for
about twenty-five or thirty leagues. In the space
of four days we crossed many brooks, and a river
(Oneida River) which proceeds from a lake (Lake
Oneida) that discharges into that of the Ento-
honorons (Ontario, again). This lake is twenty-
five or thirty leagues in circuit, contains some fine
islands, and is the place where our enemies, the
Iroquois, catch their fish, in which it abounds.[4]

The French fur trader made some contact with the
Oneidas in the early 1600's. Evidence of this lies in the
writings of the Dutchman, Herman Meyndertsz Van den
Bogaert. Van was sent by New Amsterdam authorities
in the winter of 1634-'35 to negotiate trading privileges
with the Iroquois.[5] He journeyed up the Hudson and
Mohawk and then overland as far as the Oneidas' Castle.
At this time, the Castle was situated on a hill near present-day Munnsville. From that hill, Van was treated to
a vista that included a large body of water, the Lake
Oneida, over which, the Indians told him, the Frenchmen came with goods for trade. These Frenchmen were
probably the backwoodsmen-trapper types, the kind of
men that lived close to the wilds and could deal with the
Indians. They had little to do with the bellicose Champlain. The Van den Bogaert incident gives us the first
record of Dutch penetration into the Lake Oneida region, as well as good evidence of early French ventures
into the area.

Another group of Frenchmen came to Oneida in the
1600's. These were the Jesuit missionaries, not trappers
or soldiers, but conquerors in a different sense. A local
newspaper of 1899 makes note of Father (Jacques) Bruy-

as who, in 1667, established the mission of Saint Francis
Xavier among the Oneidas.[6] A souvenir booklet for Syl-
van Beach, 1907, calls the priest "Father Bonya." Francis
Whiting Halsey, author of *The Old New York Frontier*
states, perhaps more reliably, that the priest's name was
Jacques Bruyar and that he lived among the Oneidas,
Onondagas, and Mohawks for thirty years before 1700.[7]

This Jesuit missionary was a political priest as
well. The *Ecclesiastical Records* (for the) *State of New
York* gives us the most solid clue to his identity and the
full nature of his mission to the Iroquois. A letter from
Robert Livingston, Secretary for Indian Affairs, to the
Iroquois chiefs on October 17, 1700, reads:

> ... There is a vast difference between French-
> men that come among us purely on account of
> trade, and the Popish Priests and Jesuits that
> come to deceive and delude you with their false
> doctrines and principles.
>
> I would be glad to know upon what errand or
> message it was that Mr. Marricour and Monsr.
> Bruyas, the Jesuit, and the rest of the French
> came to you lately at the Onondaga Castle ...[8]

Through Livingston's pen flows a deep distrust of Bruyas
and a suspicion of his activities. That sentiment was
shared by many more than Secretary Robert. Listen to
the Earl of Bellmont in his August 31, 1700, letter to the
Lords of Trade:

> ... I shall only observe that the message I sent
> last spring by Coll. Schuyler, Mr. Livingston and
> Mr. Hanson to The Five Nations (the Iroquois)
> was a most lucky step, and was, I may presume to
> say, hindering the Indian from a revolt to the
> French. This will appear from what the Indians
> own in page the 5th of the conference. I had the

good luck to be too nimble for Bruyas the Jesuit and Monsr. Maricour, and by my present of a belt of wampum I frustrated theirs.[9]

Father Jacques Bruyas did not limit his teaching to the Holy Gospel. It seems that the divine word of Louis XIV would do as well.

Throughout colonial history, the British and French fought for control of the Lake Oneida region. Why was this area so important? The answer to that question is a key to understanding Sylvan Beach and Lake Oneida history.

Oneida Lake, in all its years of contact with humanity, has provided a link in trade and transportation routes. Across New York, to the Saint Lawrence Valley and Canada, to the Great Lakes and the West, the colonial traveller, if he journeyed the most efficient way, went through Oneida. The path that traveler would follow across New York went like this.

Let's say our voyageur starts in New York City and makes his way to Oswego. He sails up the Hudson to Albany, makes a portage to Schenectady and enters the Mohawk. Navigation westward on the Mohawk to Rome is interrupted by but one portage, around the "little falls" at the present-day city site bearing that name. At Rome the traveler makes a significant portage from the Mohawk to Wood Creek, a small stream flowing westerly. That portage was known by several names, the "Oneida Portage," "Great Carry," "Oneida Carry," and "Carrying Place" being but a few. Once our friend casts his batteau or canoe off into the meandering Wood Creek he can journey by water to Lake Oneida, cross the lake and enter the Oneida River near present-day Brewerton. The Oneida joins the Seneca at Three Rivers' Point, the two rivers becoming the Oswego. The Oswego leads, logically, to Oswego port, on Ontario.

Branch-off points on this route gave it even greater significance. From Lake Ontario a colonial could find a water route to the Saint Lawrence and Canada, to the other Great Lakes and the undeveloped west. From Three-Rivers' Point one could journey upstream on the Seneca to the rich New York Finger Lakes region, an area of vast potential and resource. Indeed, this water route brought many pioneers to the land of the Senecas and Cayugas. It was a convenient route and convenience most rare in colonial transportation.

Difficulties in navigating this travel route were plentiful. The traveler had to depend on high water in Wood Creek, water high enough to allow boats navigation. Sluices were sometimes built to dam the creek's flow and, upon demolition, to push boats through summer shallows. In 1790, a man named Augustus Porter traveled the Wood Creek and wrote of his experience with this sluiceway navigation.

> I have heretofore remarked that the mode adopted to render Wood Creek navigable was to collect the water by means of a mill dam, thus creating a sudden flood to carry boats down. Sometimes boats did not succeed in getting through to deep water on one flood and were consequently obliged to await a second one. As we were coursing down the creek during the voyage on our first flood we overtook a boat which had grounded after the previous one, the navigators of which were in the water ready to push her off as soon as the coming tide should reach them.[10]

The low water was but one problem in navigation of this water route. Lake Oneida becomes a tempest when the west wind reaches high velocities. Waves can reach a six-foot peak in the most violent storms. To compensate for the lake's unruly nature and the quick storms which arise there, boatmen would journey along the north shore, where sheltered coves were more common and the wave effect lessened.

The Great Carry was a most important part of the route. Dollars, sweat and lives were consumed in efforts to improve and defend it. Navigation was slowed by the Carry. The portage took several hours, depending on boat size and season (more undergrowth in summer, of course). In 1796, a concrete attempt was undertaken to improve the Carry, and to eliminate the portage altogether.

For years there had been talk in Upstate about building a canal across the Carry. In 1796 this talk became reality.[11] A one and three-quarter mile long canal, linking the Mohawk with Wood Creek, was financed and built by the Western Inland Navigation Company. Boats were poled through the canal. Surprisingly enough, considering the business the Carry did, the canal did not prosper. Its construction cost was so high that tolls had to correspond and few could or would pay a high toll. People, as before, portaged, often right alongside the canal. In 1820, New York State purchased the Carrying Place Canal from Western Inland.[12] The Erie Canal of 1825 eventually occupied much of the canal's brief course.

People invested dollars in the Carry. They also invested lives. Battles were fought, forts built in the great conflicts between Britain and France and, later, Britain and the colonies. Checkmate meant control of the Carry. The moves to this end were many. All moves and the fact that these contests took place lead to one point: the Carry and the route in which it was a part were geographically and commercially important — in the North American wars, control of this route was a trump card. Here are but a few of these conflicts' highlights.

To protect this vital transportation route against the French, the English constructed a chain of forts, reaching from Albany to Oswego. In the Carry's immediate vicinity, Fort Williams, built in 1746 near present-day downtown Rome, and Fort Bull, built in 1737, were first protection.[13] Forts Newport and Stanwix were erected later, in the same area, around 1758[14]. The year 1758 also witnessed the genesis of the Royal Blockhouse (also called Fort Royal, although it was merely a blockhouse).[15] The Blockhouse rose on the south side of Wood Creek, near its entrance to Lake Oneida, across river from the site of present-day Sylvan Beach. Other forts in the British chain were Fort Brewerton (on the western tip of Lake Oneida) and Fort Oswego. As the latter two forts are out of the immediate Sylvan Beach area, we will not delve into their history, except to mention that they were essential links in the British "fort-chain" defense.

The Royal Blockhouse was virtually as immediate to Sylvan Beach as any fort could be. The fort was in planning stages for some time before its actual erection. The Sachims of the Iroquois wrote Governor Burnet, Governor of New York and New Jersey, on September 20, 1724. They protested locating the Blockhouse at its Wood Creek site.

> As to the Blockhouse it must be at the Onnondages River mouth and not at the Oneides Lake for the far Indians pass only by the mouth of the River and do not come up to the Oneides Lake so that the Beaver trap would then be so far off that it would catch no Beavers at all and this is a thing the Handlers put into your heads, on purpose that the Beavers may all go to Canada, where they would rather Trade with the French than

with you by which you may see they are not your friends.[16]

As was the case many times in American history, the Indian protests fell upon deaf ears. Their objection had no effect on the Blockhouse's destined site.

Only fifteen men garrisoned the Blockhouse—it was far from a full-sized fort. A stockade and earthen embankments enclosed the Blockhouse proper. For a while, the location of the Blockhouse was debated by amateur Upstate historians. Some thought it was on the lake-shore and others swore it was situated around the first riverbend. In 1961, J. Elet Milton of Brewerton, probably the only "Oneida Lake Historian" *per se* to ever exist, settled the dispute.[17]

Elet Milton never published much, but he wrote a paper entitled "The Royal Blockhouse at the East End of Oneida Lake." Milton, in his paper, proved that the Blockhouse was not on the lake shore. The documentarian cited, among others, Pomroy Jones, De Witt Clinton, Elkanah Watson, and Daniel Wager. His conclusive proof, however, came from a French map of the area, showing the Blockhouse's location, and from a correspondence with Houghton (Hote) Spencer, son of James Spencer, founder of Sylvan Beach.

Hote came to the Beach area in the 1840's, then a child of three or four. He used to play on the south side of Wood Creek. He, friends, and brothers played in the ruins of the Blockhouse, on the Creek's south side, around the first bend from the lake. Hote fondly remembered his youthful frolics on the site of that French and Indian War relic.

There were probably more like Hote, if Milton could have found them. People wanting to talk about their past—maybe they knew something about that Blockhouse. Many Sylvan Beachers will talk with you about their history.

That same Sylvan Beach Blockhouse finds its place in renown military history. Francis Parkman, author of *The Conspiracy of Pontiac,* mentions the Blockhouse in his tracing of the New York water transportation route. Parkman writes:

> . . . Then crossing overland to Wood Creek, he (the traveler) would follow its tortuous course, overshadowed by the dense forest on its banks, until he arrived at the little fortification called the Royal Blockhouse, and the waters of the Oneida Lake spread before him.[18]

The Royal Blockhouse never saw great military action. It was an outpost, a post between forts. The Blockhouse burned on March 12, 1767. A letter from a Rd. Aylmer to Sir William Johnson dated March 16 of that year gives an account of the event.

> A man arrived at this place (Fort Stanwix) two days ago, who informed me that on the 12th, at night, the Royal Blockhouse took fire and was immediately consumed to ashes; the fire (he said) first took in some of the logs near the chimney by its being much worn away — there had been three Senecas, two Oneidas, a frenchman and three squaws in the house at the time, who had lost all their packs in the flames, by the accident being so unexpected and so very furious, even their dogs were burnt.[19]

The Blockhouse was falling into a state of disuse even before 1767. Wood Creek eventually eroded its earthen foundations, causing the remainder of the fort to capsize into the stream. By the late 1880's, nothing remained.

Though Sylvan Beach's immediate vicinity was left

relatively untouched by the French and Indian Wars, the Oneida Lake and Great Carry area as a whole saw much military action. What follows is but a sketch of happenings of this era — a full military history is impossible and inappropriate here. It would stretch for pages on end and would certainly be out of character with Sylvan Beach's history, the central theme of this work.

Armies maneuvered and battled over the Carrying Place, Wood Creek and Lake Oneida. In 1755, Colonel John Bradstreet, a man "noted for his vigor and celerity," crossed the Carry with soldiers and supplies for Oswego, in a record time of three hours (Guinness, take note).[20] Upon reaching Oneida, Bradstreet was attacked by Indians, but emerged victorious from the conflict, slaying a reported two hundred of the foe while losing thirty of his company.

In March of 1756, the French General DeLery, with Indian allies, attacked and destroyed Fort Bull. The fort's garrison resisted little and suffered dearly. A French account of the battle reads as follows:

> The detachment having commenced their march along the highroad, the soldiers having their bayonets fixed, M. DeLery gave orders to move straight forward without firing a shot and seize the guard on entering the fort. He was still five acres off when he heard the whoop of the Indians, not withstanding the prohibition he had issued. He instantly ordered an advance, double quick time, in order to carry the gate of the fort, but the enemy had time to close it .... Our soldiers and the Canadians, who ran full speed, the moment the Indians whooped, got possession of the holes; through these they fired on such of the English as they could get sight of. Great efforts

were made to batter down the gate, which was finally cut to pieces in about an hour. Then the whole detachment, with a cry "Vive le Roi!" rushed into the fort and put everyone to the sword they could lay hands on. One woman and a few soldiers were fortunate to escape the fury of our troops.[21]

Fearing the arrival of reinforcements with Sir William Johnson, the British "Indian Diplomat" of the Mohawk Valley, the French retreated the next day, throwing much of their plunder into Wood Creek.

The primary purpose of DeLery's attack was to disturb British ammunition and supply traffic over the Carry. The Frenchman succeeded. Note DeLery's list of captured supplies:

Fourty thousand weight of powder, a number of bombs, grenades, and balls of different calibre. A great deal of salted provisions, bread, butter, chocolate, sugar and other provisions were likewise thrown into the water. The stores were filled with clothes and other effects which were pillaged; the remainder burned.[72]

DeLery's attack disrupted English plans, but it did not diminish the importance of the Carry as a trump card in the war. Gilbert Hagerty, contemporary historian of the Fort Bull "massacre," analyzed the effect of DeLery's raid on the Carry's prominence. Mr. Hagerty postulated:

Oneida Carry, the short stretch of road along the swamp between the Mohawk River and Wood Creek, still remained the essential tie between the lakes (Great Lakes) and the sea, as it had through Colonial times. One large post, Fort Stanwix, was yet to be built in 1758 to protect the Carry

through the remainder of the French war; and
in the dark years following, an even greater drama
of agony, courage, and sacrifice would be played
out under its ramparts.[23]

The Carry had to remain important; it was a cog in a
primary westward route.

In March of 1756, General William Shirley of Oswego was relieved by a supply convoy that crossed Lake
Oneida on the ice.[24] August of that year saw the capture
of Oswego by the French.[25] At that time, General Daniel
Webb was marching to the fort's aid and learned, on
reaching the Carry, that he was too late. Webb retreated
down the Mohawk, but before falling back, he directed his
men to fell trees into Wood Creek. When the French ad-
vanced, they were compelled to clear the creek of obstruc-
tions. According to legend, the French gave Wood Creek
its name (Riviere du Chicot—River of Stumps) because
of this incident. This is, however, a legend, but legends
serve a fine purpose of making history colorful.

The Revolutionary War enlivened military activity
in the Oneida Lake region. General Barry St. Leger and
his troops travelled through the area on their way to
Stanwix and Oriskany, where they met frustration at
the hands of Nicholas Herkimer's colonial irregulars.
In April of 1779, Colonel Goose Van Schaik and a
Colonel Willett, as a part of the famous Sullivan campaign against the Iroquois allies of England, led an ex-
pedition from Stanwix to Brewerton, via Wood Creek
and Oneida.[26] After destroying some Onondaga towns,
the soldiers returned via the same route, spending a night
on Frenchman's Island, an isle of Oneida.

To cite more military incidents of the area's history
at this point would prove fruitless. The local struggles of
the French and Indian and Revolutionary wars illustrated the importance of the east-west transportation

route, of which Lake Oneida and Wood Creek were integral parts. To control this route meant control of a major highway, a turnpike if you will, of North America. Throughout our history, Lake Oneida has been an important link in transportation for this country, as well as for New York State. The lake's colonial history is but one part of the chain of events and facts that prove Oneida's geographical importance. The lake's location and inherent resources profoundly affected upstate history and, of course, the history of Sylvan Beach.

Sylvan Beach, in its history, has had several names.

The papers of a Captain Machin, a member of the Sullivan Campaign, have been passed on to us today. A paper dated April 19, 1779, contains this entry:

> Early on Monday morning, 19th April, 1779 —marched from Fort Schuyler (near present day Utica) with a detachment of troops consisting of 558 men including officers and after marching (putting) eight days provisions in batteaux which had been conveyed over the carrying place in the night, and leaving a sufficient number of soldiers to assist the batteausmen to get the boats down Wood Creek, with five officers to hurry them on— the remainder of the troops marched to the 'old scow place' (my quotes), 21 miles by land, but much more by water. The troops arrived at 3 o'clock P.M., but the boats did not arrive until 10 o'clock, having been much obstructed by trees which had fallen across the creek. As soon as the boats arrived, the whole of the troops embarked, and on entering the Onidahogo (Lake Oneida) was much impeded by a cold head wind.[27]

The "old scow place" was, without a doubt, near the point where Wood Creek joined Lake Oneida. The geographical facts given about its location by Machin leave no room for conjecture. This name, the "old scow place," is the first documented name for the immediate Sylvan Beach area. The name certainly implies that more than one batteau or canoe found Sylvan Beach, its lake and its river, a watery grave.

People traveled through Lake Oneida and wrote about what they saw. Some people described — they recorded very objective descriptions of what surrounded them. Others wrote in purely subjective terms — they dreamed, romanticized, wrote about aesthetics — the region was, and still is, very beautiful country.

I enjoy listening to these people — they are talking about an area that I know so well, but that they knew at a different time. Let's hear what they have to say. First, the objective describers:

William Johnson, in his diary, 1761:

Saturday October 24.

Rained this morning, and from 12 o'clock last night, so I hope the water will be good in Wood Creek. Ordered the boats ready to embark. Very raw, cold, and wet weather. I was full of pain all last night from my old wound. Embarked at 9 o'clock. Wind turned ahead after we got about eight miles into the lake, and continued so all the day. Arrived at the royal block house at the E. end of Oneida Lake after sunset. Went to the fort and supped with Captain Baw, Gray, and Mr. Burns. At 8 o'clock went to camp and drank a few glasses of Madeira with Mr. Burns & c. and went to bed as usual.[28]

A very "matter-of-fact" account of a trip through the area. Johnson wrote about what he did, not about the beauty around him.

Ralph Izard, a friend of George Washington (he probably met him in one of the places where he reputedly "slept") and future South Carolina senator, traveled westward from New York to Niagara in June of 1765. He passed through Lake Oneida.

> Monday 14th — Went on horseback by the side of Wood Creek 20 miles to the Royal blockhouse, a kind of wooden castle, proof against any Indian attacks. It is now abandoned by the troops and a settler lives there, who keeps rum, milk, and racoons, which though nothing of the most elegant, is comfortable to the strangers passing that way. This block house is situated at the east end of Oneida Lake, and is surrounded by the Oneida, one of the Six Nations. Some of our batteaux not being come up, we stayed the next day at the blockhouse.

> 16th — Embarked and rowed to the west end of the lake which is 28 miles, to Fort Brewington (Brewerton), a small stockade, built in the last war. The Oneida Lake is 20 miles from north to south.[29]

Like Johnson, Izard was a writer who described his trip, in purely empirical terms. He was also a very inaccurate estimator. Oneida is at most five miles from north to south.

The French and Indian Wars brought many travelers through the Lake Oneida-Wood Creek region. One such person was a French spy, scouting the territory. As one might suspect, the spy's reports were detailed descriptions of what he saw. This particular document dates from November 28, 1757.

> Lake Oneida is twelve leagues long and about one league wide. Its navigation is beautiful and

practicable at all times, unless there be a strong contrary wind. It is best on the right side of the lake, which is on the north side.

From Lake Oneida we enter the River Vilcrick (Wood Creek) which empties into that lake, and ascend nine leagues to Fort Bull. This river is full of sinuosities, narrow and sometimes embarrassed with trees fallen from both banks. Its navigation is difficult when water is low. It is, however, passable at all times with ordinary bateau load of 14 to 1,500 weight. When the waters of this stream are low, an ordinary bateau load cannot go by the river further than a league of Fort Bull. It becomes necessary then to unload and make a carrying place of the remainder by the road constructed to the Fort, or to send back the bateau for the other half load.

Fort Bull, which was burnt in 1756 by a detachment under the orders of M. de Lery, was situated on the right bank of this river near its source, on the height of land.[30]

The "matter-of-fact" style of Johnson and Izard knew no national boundaries. Frenchmen could delve into plain description with seemingly equal ease.

Many others described, but descriptions lack the colour of the words of the dreamer, the romantic. It is to the latter world that we now travel.

Elkanah Watson, along with Jeremiah Van Rensslaer, General Philip Van Cortlandt, and Stephen Bayard, toured upstate in 1791. Sections of Watson's account of that journey read:

Immediately after breakfast we embarked, doubled a point of land, and entered the Oneida Lake with our sails filled to a light easterly breeze. The lake opened to our view, spreading before us like a sea. We glided smoothly over its surface, and were delighted with a charming day . . . This lake is thirty miles long and from five to eight broad. We are now sailing parallel with the Ontario ocean, which I hope to see, and at least enjoy in delightful anticipation the open water communication from thence to the Atlantic, via Albany and New York.

In giving a stretch to the mind into futurity, I saw those fertile regions, bounded west by the Mississippi, north by the great lakes, east by the Allegany mountains, and south by the placid Ohio, overspread with millions of freemen; blessed with various climates, enjoying every variety of soil, and commanding the boldest inland navigation on this globe . . . [31]

Watson's mind overflowed with dreams. He recognized the potential growth and importance of the area and of New York State as a thoroughfare. Watson wrote of Wood Creek and its canal-like qualities.

From a superficial view of this important creek, it appears to me, the great difficulties (in navigation) may be surmounted: first, by cutting away all the bushes and trees on its banks; second, by cutting across the necks, and removing all sunken logs and trees; and lastly by erecting substantial sluices or inclined planes, at given distances, so as to continue a head of water from sluice to sluice. This creek, in its present state, may be considered a natural canal, from ten to twenty feet wide . . .

. . . Should the western canals ever be attempted, I am persuaded that this creek may be shortened at least one-third.[32]

Elkanah Watson saw the potential for westward expansion in New York. Canals occupied an integral part in his expansion scheme. Watson viewed the Wood Creek thoroughfare, then the most important travel route, but did not commit himself to it as *the* canal pathway. There were alternatives for the great canal and, eventually, an alternative became that canal's site.

Another man came through the area, three years afterward, and settled on the lake's north shore. He was Francis Adrian Van Der Kemp; he saw much in Lake Oneida and its country.

> Both Salmon rivers emptying in Lake Ontario, to the north of this tract of land and the Fish creek in Oneida Lake are, in the spring and fall, full of salmon. One Oneida Indian took with his spear forty-five salmon in one hour. They are equal to the best that are caught in the rivers of the Rhine and Meuse . . .
>
> This country, so abundant in water and fish is, if possible, yet more profusely endowed by our bountiful maker with wood. Every kind of timber of the northern and eastern states is here in the greatest plenty and perfection.[33]

Van Der Kemp's words flow with enthusiasm for his new found home. Not all was pleasant, however, as he learned from his encounter with the infamous eel-fly of Oneida. It totally ruined his fishing.

> We have now lost a great part of two days in fishing, without an adequate reward to our exertions, and might have suspected that the exuberant abundance of this lake in fish, of which we had heard so much boasting from white men as well as Indians, had been exaggerated, but soon we discovered the cause of our failure. The

lake was now covered as with a white cloak of
hundreds, thousands, millions of insects which
we call Haft in Holland, and which lay in some
parts of the shore one and two inches deep.[34]

Throughout Sylvan Beach history, the eel-fly has plagued
people. Sometimes the flies would be so plentiful that
cars would need their bright lights in broad daylight.
Beach residents even used snow shovels to clear flies off
the sidewalks and streets.

Van Der Kemp selected a site near present-day Constantia for his home. The town of Rotterdam eventually
grew in the immediate vicinity. Van Der Kemp wrote
of his land:

> . . . here was the land to some extent towards the
> lake low, and could only be appropriated for pas-
> ture or hay land; but it gradually ascended about
> 20 feet, where it was covered with a deep, black,
> rich, fertile soil, mixed with a small portion of
> black sand, and covered with majestic oak, beech,
> butternut, walnut, ash and maple . . . Imagine
> that falling plain near the lake, cleared from trees
> and stumps, and covered with verdure, embel-
> lished with a dozen of cows, the lake in front, a
> wood to the south, while behind you the noblest
> fields invite you to admire the rich produce of the
> soil, equal to the best tilled in our country.[35]

The man was impressed.

Francis Adrian Van Der Kemp did not spend his
remaining years on Oneida. In 1797, he and his family
migrated to Olden-barneveld, north of present-day Utica.
He died there in 1829.[36] Prior to his death, he served
Governor DeWitt Clinton in research for the Erie Canal,
the waterway that would cause so great a boom in upstate New York.

Van Der Kemp and Watson realized the potential of the Oneida region. Their writings abound with ideas for developing the region's vast resources.

George Scriba, an affluent New York businessman, attempted to develop the Lake Oneida region in the late 18th and early 19th centuries. Scriba, a Dutchman, emigrated to the United States around the revolutionary era, settled in New York, prospered through economic acumen and eventually became a founder of the Bank of New York. He was a staunch Federalist, an elite man, friend to Hamilton, John Jay and Philip Schuyler. In 1790 his fortune was reputed to the tune of one and one-half million dollars.

On December 12, 1794, Scriba received a patent for New York frontier land between the north shore of Lake Oneida and the southeast shore of the Lake Ontario. He appointed Benjamin Wright, a noted surveyor, to divide the tract into townships and to determine exact acre count. Wright's 1794 plotting attributed 525,063 acres and twenty-four townships to Scriba ownership. In the patent agreement, Scriba assented to pay for a sixth of the land within six months, one-half of the remainder within a year, and the rest within two years. Total land costs reached into six-figure dollar counts.

George Scriba's life knew great success and deep tragedy. Sadly, the latter found manifestation in Scriba's Lake Oneida area ventures. What follows now is a concise, diary-biography of George Scriba, a narration of several poignant episodes in his New York frontier experience. Listen to the man as he speaks here; let his words take you in the first person to history and an American dream.[37]

New York City, 1790.

A merchant's life in this great and new city gives one nary a moment for rest and contemplation. Orders, orders, goods coming in and going out, this surely must be the price of prosperity. My enterprise now attracts buyers from even as far as New Haven, notably the worthy Mr. Hotchkiss who purchases opium and drugs from my stores. Without the sturdy packet boats what would this merchant become? An enclosed Shylock on the streets of trade? Perhaps a resourceful, soured Yankee, the business equal of any man, but without any sense of humor and vivacity. Still, though, dealing with them keeps the mind keen. There is much to be admired in their character.

The name of this land's brief history has been "expansion." Look at friend Hamilton and his plans for economic solidarity; from there who knows what could happen? There is already expansion into the previously savaged hinterlands and only divine providence knows what prosperity might arise if the untapped resources of those lands find linkage to the teeming trading ports of this coast. An inland empire attends those daring enough to risk life and fortune for its development.

I believe that I am such a man. George Scriba, the New York frontier awaits your gilded touch. "New York." Even the name rings with civilization's bounty. No lesser person could accomplish what you will create. Scriba, Scriba, Scriba, Scriba . . . you will write your name in history.

Sailing North on the Hudson
April, 1792

Visions of futurity, extrapolated from the reality of empire: I have acquired some half-million acres of virgin land. Soil is reputed excellent, timber they say is there of the finest quality. The rivers run deep from and to the lakes, carrying an overabundance of fishes. Waterpower from streams will never be lacking. Winters are reported harsh, but that is but one of four seasons.

We sail onward now, through the narrow section of this river the boatmen call the "highlands." This river is deep-run to Albany, providing superb channels of navigation. From the latter town we journey westward along the Mohawk's river to a place they call the "Carry" and from thence down the Wood Creek to my Lake Oneida. It is not mine, but it is a main route through this country and, as it forms part of a southern border to my lands, it can but assist in their blossom. My territories also include the Ontario ocean, a lake in actuality though a very large one, which carries commerce from Canada to the west. Thus, my estate situates at the crossroads to two great inland waterways, blessed with innumerable resources.

If expansion is the name of America, I cannot help but know it. Destiny thy name is Scriba.

Rotterdam, Oneida Lake
December, 1794

We have begun, in a small but calculated scale, the task of development. Mr. Wright has surveyed my acreage and divided it into twenty-four towns, each being itself separated into individual lots. Rotterdam, on Oneida's northwest shore near the mouth of Bruce's creek, will provide ideal location for my central land office, as settlers must pass through or near the town on their way to other parts of my land.

I shall soon begin establishment of my Ontario port, to be named Vera Cruz. It shall be situated near the mouth of the Salmon Creek, a perfect harbor for the port that shall rival and eventually surpass Oswego in commercial prominence.

All ambition must wait through this season, however, as climate and personal absence postpone immediate progress. I must return to New York for payment on my land, and to attend the merchant's life, which I shall soon abandon to direct affairs here. Wirth and Mang will manage Rotterdam while I am gone. They are able men, perhaps a bit rash and temper given, but they are my most trusted, save Van der Kemp, at this time. I must rely on them.

New York
January, 1795

Disappointment knocks at the new year's door. Reports filter through from the patent that Messrs. Wirth and Mang betray my trust. They govern my land with abandon, dictating rent and credit policies that I could never conceive. They have proved lax in building my mill dam. They use my oxen for their enterprise, these arrogant and demanding men! I pray that our salted pork and flour supplies have not met with their mismanagement. My people need assurance of basics through this winter. At the infant stage of empire all must be done to insure that what settlers I have remain on the frontier.

Tyrants I will never have at my place. I see now that all management rests in my hand alone. In time, a man must learn that his most trusted and reliable friend is always himself.

Rotterdam
June, 1795

I am encouraged. My gristmill is now five stories, functional to the ultimate and probably the largest in this upstate country. Over thirty souls have used it during this pay period, enough to create a healthy circulation of capital. And the names, the fantastic diversity of names that have come to me, first for land, now to grind the fruits of the land. Cornelius Van Winkle, Betsey Van Rippen, Jean Louraine, William Barbour, Molly McCracken, John Ford, Gideon Bowden. These are the first of the many who will build my empire.

A blanketed Oneida Indian barters away his furs at the Scriba store. His mink, otter and beaver will bring excellent prices in the city markets. Along the north shore of this lake stretch settlements of single families, soon to be linked as more colonists arrive. Two of these, Mr. Van der Kemp and Mr. Bernhard, provide excellent company, the former for his learning, the latter for his most amusing character. James Bernhard is no fine pioneer, devoid of the common senses one must have to prevail in this country. His spirit needs calming and I fear it may bring misfortune. One cannot plow a wave without sinking.

That Frenchman, a Duke he called himself, proved an interesting sidelight yesterday. The poor, shiftless traveller was looking at America, catching a quick look I would imagine, as his cultured arse appeared to have the greatest ache. Liancourt, yes, that was the man. He seemed to take a liking to DesWattines, another "prise de la nation francaise." DesWattines, for one of noble birth, has adjusted well to the rigors of this life. Still, he is so disagreeably condescending that few but his wife can stand his company for over an hour. Frenchmen are continual players in this American tragicomedy I call survival. They play aloof fools.

* * * * *

This first "aloof fool" Scriba mentioned was the Duke De La Rochefaucault Liancourt, on a tour of North America. Liancourt wrote of Scriba and his Rotterdam.

Rotterdam is an infant settlement, formed but ten months ago. Mr. Schreiber (Scriba), a rich Dutch merchant, possesses a large tract of land extending from Lake Ontario to Lake Oneida. He fixed upon the mouth of Bruce Creek as the site of the chief place, and another settlement he has formed on Little Salmon Creek, two miles from

Lake Ontario . . . Mr. Schreiber has made a road
from Rotterdam to his new town, but all these
settlements are yet of no importance. The whole
city of Rotterdam, to which the founder has given
its name in honor of his native place, consists of
about twenty houses.

. . . The land which eight months ago he purchased for one dollar an acre, costs now three, but
is not much sought after. The present settlers
come from New England and the environs of
Albany.[38]

Perhaps this outsider wrote with objectivity. His and
Scriba's viewpoints differed greatly. Where lies the accurate picture? We now examine what happened to the
empire as it matured.

*   *   *   *   *

Rotterdam, 1798
Year's advent

Oh I am hurried this day! We have a post office, the
first post office of the region. This essential institution
I have sorely missed, to say nothing of my settlers' wants.
As the mails bring the outside world closer, they truly
must enhance the value and development potential of
my lands. With joy I will place the Scriba seal on a letter
this day and mail it . . . at the Rotterdam, at my, post
office.

This joy be so welcome, so welcome indeed. I am still
at a loss for Van der Kemp. He, his wife and even the
Negro wench he possessed were a constant reminder of
the good things our civilization begets. These were dig-
nified Dutchmen, cognizant of the greatness inherent in
my lands, of the nobility this country embraces. They
were my friends, and still are, but they no longer live by
my side. I shall miss them.

* * * * *

It is difficult to speak in terms of omens, good or bad, with any degree of accuracy, but Van der Kemp's departure from the Scriba patent cannot be construed as anything but a negative sign. Van der Kemp shared Scriba's zeal for the land probably more than any other settler. To his death, he continued in this feeling, but he left the land he loved and praised. It seems that there was more opportunity elsewhere.

By 1807 Scriba had $300,000 remaining from his initial fortune. His empire was debt ridden. Many colonists passed through his region, yet they did not settle there. Domestic issues within the nation and the patent combined to rip Scriba's spirit and fortune until little of the original man remained. We shall see what became of this once proud, confident Ozimandias.

* * * * *

November 1820

I have nothing left from my riches. All investments have resulted in nil. My townships do anything but thrive and, with the building of the canal people talk about, travellers will no longer use the Lake Oneida in numbers. "No immediate chance for growth" — the phrase will be an epitaph. Mr. David Parish, my principal creditor, has agreed to repossess my property, leaving me my home and several lots for my use and my son's, upon my death. People call that security. It is nothing but misfortune's hell. A token for a poor man.

I keep writing "Constantia, Constantia, Constantia, Constantia." This is what they call my Rotterdam. The word is a grand discord designed to haunt me for my remaining life. What is there for me now but memory? So little value that word has, at least for me. Memory only conjures the image of what could have been. It is the pauper's fate, the rich man's constant friend.

April 1822
Constantia

Must I be reduced to a subject for charity? Friend Van der Kemp writes me today, "his dear and respected friend," a man of the "noble mind." Francis Adrian's words I value, but they offer little consolation. Instead he brings through them the offer of a gift. "If fifty dollars can be of service to you towards the fall . . . tell only how I shall make the payment." Van der Kemp has done well for himself, what with his work on canals for the governor. He must be comfortable at Oldenbarneveld.

I can nary say the same. We are but townspeople now, as common as the rest. Oh, there are rumors of Scriba and his wealth that circulate through this country, but what are these but ghosts of nightmare? There is no one here I can call friend, save family. Even myself I doubt with a severity that would bend the stiffest critic's tongue. My youthful vigor and dream are now but a reminder of what could have been.

With the building of the canal, New York will grow and prosper like no other state. The canal will so facilitate westward commerce that the old trade route through my territory will suffer through disuse. Rotterdam and these lake villages, though, have not seen their zenith! There will be a boom here, but I will never prosper from it. Scriba, Scriba, you dream again. Dream on old man. It's the only saving grace remaining. To sleep, perchance . . .

*   *   *   *   *

1836
Constantia

I look now to review my past.

In the year 1794 the first tree was cut down and I began to clear a few acres of land on the Oneida Lake, where the village of Constantia is now located. I directed my then agent major to have three log houses built, one

for myself as a temporary dwelling and one for a boarding house for my laborers and one for a family to cook.
I also erected a sawmill this year on Bruce's Creek, since
Scriba's Creek. In 1795 and 1796 I erected two two-story
houses and a barn and stables, one for my temporary
occupation and also for the occupation of my agent and
his family. The other was for a tavern. Also, ten small
houses for the accommodation of mechanics and their
families were built that year. A large building for a flour-
ing mill calculated to take four tons of stone was begun
that year. Finally, a store was established with goods for
a trading company, intended for carrying on inland commerce and the fur trade with the west. Another such store
was established at Salmon Creek, on Lake Ontario.

Through the settlers in the town of Mexico, trading
began with Kingston in Upper Canada and elsewhere on
Lake Ontario. A disaster had taken place in November
('96). A certain Captain Gurmann, an enterprising man
who had built a schooner on Salmon Creek, Mexico, went
with five men, himself and a boy to Kingston. On their
return they were cast away and never afterwards heard
of. Thus the disaster deprived the infant settlement of
enterprising and industrious citizens and left behind a
number of unfortunate families in great distress.

The winter set in with its usual severity. As soon as I
was informed of the disaster, I ordered my agent to send
sufficient provisions for the relief of those widows and
orphans. This disaster occasioned a general gloom over
the settlement at Mexico.

Times, in general, began to look gloomy. Emigration
was not so rapid. Money grew less. The settlers could not
pay either interests in arrears or principal according to
contract. In order to keep them on the land longer time
was given them. Many sold out. Instead of land prices
rising, they fell from fifty to one hundred percent. Taxes

and road making required more capital than could be collected.

As time passed, through embargoes and all sorts of restrictive measures, we were at the verge of war with Great Britain. During that war, all our frontier settlements on the lakes, particularly Lake Ontario, were abandoned and settlers returned to more secure places. Many never returned to the frontier. This, of course, was very injurious for the country and for myself. That war became very disastrous during its continuance. Commerce was crippled. The cultivator felt it bearing hard upon him. Farming produce fell from fifty to two hundred percent in price. Labor costs had risen.

The militia were called out to guard our state's frontier. All of these factors combined to produce a general stagnation in this western part in all business.

The national government's finances were ruined by this war. Credit had sunk to a new low. The government had to borrow much money to carry out its war and now I could not obtain loans without paying high interest rates. This disasterous state of affairs lasted until after peace had been made and a national bank could be established and begin its operation. Since 1822, there has not been another part of this world that has prospered so much as these United States.

*   *   *   *   *

But stability came too late. George Scriba's day had passed. His time was simply the wrong one.

George Scriba had sound ideas for development, but he was born at the wrong time. He chose a superb area for expansion, but domestic problems within his patent and the nation as a whole worked against him. There was immigration during Scriba's years, but settlers passed through his region. Scriba's soil was not ideal for farming, and farming was the interest of most western colonists. Scriba's area's resources—fish, timber, water power, recreational assets — were to reach their peak development in later years.

Scriba's ambition and dreams were later taken up by men who built Sylvan Beach and the resorts that encircled Lake Oneida. They brought out potential in the lake — they finished Scriba's task. Had George Scriba invested his fortune in the lake area in the late 1800's, he probably would have prospered. He didn't, though, but his name lives on, in the "Scriba Creek," on historical markers of Constantia village, in numerous deeds and land transactions, and in that American god, idol, and ideal that we call enterprise.

* * * * *

Timothy Dwight, President of Yale and controversial theologian of the early nineteenth century, made a journey to Niagara in 1804. Dwight never touched on the Oneida shores but in the Sullivan township he viewed the lake from a hill top.

> In the township of Sullivan, a large tract lying immediately eastward of Manlius, we found, however, an exception (to the thick forests which covered the countryside).
>
> As we descended a hill of considerable height, we were presented with a delightful prospect of the Oneida Lake, and a noble view of the circum jacent country.[39]

"Delightful" was the word and the sentiment. Dwight also gives an interesting note of an encounter between Samuel Kirkland, founder of Hamilton College, and Lake Oneida.

> Mr. Kirkland informed me that while he was crossing the Oneida Lake with a fleet of canoes, a violent storm arose, from which the fleet was in

the utmost danger of perishing. The chief sachem, in whose canoe Mr. Kirkland was, took a box in the stern a small quantity of fine powder made of a fragrant herb unknown to Mr. Kirkland and scattered it on the water. This he found was intended as an oblation to the deity acknowledged by the sachem.[40]

Kirkland easily could have perished in that canoe during an Oneida gale. He was lucky to have the Indians as friends.

DeWitt Clinton, one of the most influential governors in New York history, went on a western canal trip in 1810. Clinton was examining possible routes for canals through the state. In his journey he visited Oneida and wrote:

> We arrived at Mrs. Jackson's tavern, at seven o'clock, near the mouth of Wood Creek, which enters Oneida Lake from the north-east. To the west, the eye was lost in the expanse of waters, there being no limits to the horizon. A western wind gently agitated the surface of the waters. A number of canoes darting through the lake after fish in a dark night, with lighted flambeaux of pine knots fixed on elevated iron frames, made a very picturesque and pleasing exhibition. We walked on the beach, composed of the finest sand, like the shores of the ocean, and covered with a few straggling trees.[41]

"Very picturesque," "pleasing," a beach "composed of the finest sand." DeWitt Clinton appreciated what he saw.

Lake Oneida is eutrophic, an aging lake. Eutrophication comes from the minerals and nutrients in the soil drained by Oneida's feeder streams. People often mistake the eutrophic algae in the lake for pollution— nothing could be further from the truth. Clinton mused about this algae, the "lake blossom."

> The waters of the lake were saturated with small dark atoms, which render them unsalubrious, and when drank, operate emetically, and produce fever. This, in the language of the boatmen, is termed the lake blossom. Whether it arises from   the farina of the chestnut, or any other trees that blossom about this time . . . we could not determine . . . If I were to give an opinion, it would be that it is not an animal substance, but small atoms swept into the lake by the waters of Wood Creek, from the vegetable putrefactions generated in the swamps and marshes through which that stream runs.[42]

Pollution? History refuted any such statement.

Near the western extremity of Oneida floats an island, named the "Frenchman's Island." Lake boatmen knew the island as "Hoger Bust" or "high breast" — its reefs and shallow surrounding waters undoubtedly caused many a grounding.[43] Locals today talk of the snakes of Frenchman's — and there are many. The island and the person for whom it was named provides us with one of the most romantic stories of Lake Oneida.

Van der Kemp visited Hoger Bust and painted its portrait for us with these words:

> This island might in ancient days have been the happy seat of a goddess, in the middle age that of a magician, or a fairy's residence in the times of chivalry. Proceeding on one after another through the stately trees, through which we perceived yet the last glances of the setting sun, we were at once, after a few yards, surprised with an

enchanting view, of which it is not in my power to
give you an adequate description. All that the
poets did sing of the gardens of Alurions, all the
scenery of those of Armeida, so highly decorated
by Virgil and Aristo, could scarce have been made
upon me, who was captivated unaware and be-
wildered, a more deep impression than this spec-
tacle of nature. We did see here a luxuriant soil in
its virgin bloom; we did see industry crowned
with blessing, we did see here what great things a
frail man can perform if he is willing. It seemed
a paradise which happiness had chosen for her
residence.[44]

Clinton, in his diary, tells of the Frenchman of Lake
Oneida:

One of the islands (in the lake) is called the
Frenchman's Island, from a person of that nation, who took possession of it about fifteen years
ago, with a beautiful wife. He resided there until
the cold weather came, and then he wintered in
Albany, Rome, or Rotterdam. He had a handsome collection of books, musical instruments,
and all the appendages of former opulence and re-
finement.

. . . We are told by Mrs. Stevens, that his name
was Devity or Devitzy . . .[45]

The identity of that Frenchman has been a topic for
much conjecture. Van der Kemp met the man and his
wife and noted:

They lived there without servants, without
neighbors, without a cow; they lived, as it were,
separated from the world. Des Wattines sallied
forward and gave us a cordial welcome in his des-
menes. The well-educated man was easily recog-

nized through his sloven dress ... A female, from
whose remaining beauties might be conjectured
how many had been tarnished by adversity, was
sitting in the entrance of this cot.[46]

The Frenchman had an aristocratic background. He
and his wife lived alone on the island for several years,
but later hunger forced them inland to Rotterdam. They
had a child, a daughter Camille, while living on the island. Camille was the first white child born in Oswego
County.

Alexis de Tocqueville visited the island in 1832. The
story of the Frenchman inspired his mind and imagination.

We then felt certain that we were on the very
spot chosen, forty years ago, by our two unfortunate countrymen, as their last asylum. But even
by digging in the thick layers of leaves which covered the ground we could find only a few fragments
falling into dust, and which will soon disappear.
Of the remains of her who had not feared to exchange the pleasures of civilized life for a tomb
in a desert island in the New World, we could not
find a trace. Did the exile leave these precious
relics in the desert; or did he remove them to the
spot wither he went to end his days? No one could
tell us.[67]

The Frenchman's name was Des Watines. Several
sources, Van der Kemp and La Rochefaucault Liancourt, closely agree on that point. Rochefaucault, during
his previously mentioned journey to America, met the
"DesVatines" family after they had moved from the
island to Rotterdam. Adam Mappa, a Rotterdam resident, had given Des Watines a farm. Rochefaucault reports Des Watines as being "a man of some distinction,"

having claimed that "he possessed a viscount's estate in the neighborhood of Lisle." His prestige around Rotterdam was limited to having the "reputation of being a very skillful gardiner." DesWatines described himself as a "prodigal' 'to Rochefaucault — the latter thought the Frenchman to be of a rather immature, unstable nature. The Duke wrote, "By his own confession the various changes of his place of residence have been regulated by the inconsistency of his character, rather than by mature deliberation."

Rochefaucault's Des Watines was a very unhappy man. He hated Americans, thinking they all cheat in business transactions and are "extremely dull and melancholy." He considered Rotterdam people to be worse than all other Americans and, to show his contempt, sold produce to them at the "highest possible rate." Des Watines' wife was "as little pleased with America as her husband, especially the environs of Lake Oneida."[48]

Contrast Rochefaucault's tale with DeTocqueville's visions of the Frenchman and you can understand how stories about that man's identity and character have become confused. Contrast those impressions with the following, most far-fetched story about the Frenchman and all will be clear. This saga comes to us via an historical and statistical gazeteer for New York, 1860. This story not only stretches the imagination, but defies credibility. People believed it, though . . .

> During the French Revolution of 1793, when the French nobility were compelled to seek safety in flight, and the trains of exiles to this country were crowded with dukes and princes of the blood, the Count St. Hilary, a young Frenchman, and his beautiful and accomplished wife, the daughter of the noble house of Clermont, landed upon our shores. Following the trail of emigration west-

ward, they reached Oneida Lake, then on the great thoroughfare of travel; and, attracted by the beautiful island and its primitive forests, they landed upon it, and concluded to make it their future home. Here, in the deep solitude of nature, they enjoyed for many months perfect peace and quietude. Their place of residence was at length discovered by Chancellor Livingston, who had formerly enjoyed the elegant hospitalities of the lady's family at Paris. He visited them in their rural home and, after spending some time with them, he prevailed upon them to return to his mansion upon the Hudson. There they continued to reside until Bonaparte had put an end to the reign of terror and restored much of the confiscated property to the exiles of the Revolution, when they returned to France. Several years after as Livingston stood upon the banks of the Seine, amidst a crowd of distinguished Parisians, to witness the first experiment of Robert Fulton in steam navigation, he was recognized by the count, who at once took him to his residence, and treated him during his stay at Paris as a generous benefactor and an honored guest. Livingston's mansion upon the Hudson and the first steamboat of Fulton and Livingston were both named, in honor of the lady's family, 'Clermont.'[49]

What fools and lofty dreamers be the mortals who imagined that saga. Livingston's "Clermont" estate was named long before Fulton began work on his steamboat. Any tie-in with the Lake Oneida Frenchman is purely fictional.

T. Wood Clarke, in his work *Emigres In The Wilderness,* presents the most rational approach to the Frenchman's identity that this author encountered. Mr. Clarke makes clear distinction between myth and fact. He wrote:

> Concerning this early settler of what is still known as Frenchman's Island in Oneida Lake, there are many romantic traditions, most of them probably untrue. M. Devatines (variation of Des-Vatines or DesWattines, a variation to be expected) was certainly a French gentleman of culture and learning. One rumor has it that he was an aristocrat who had escaped the Reign of Terror. Another is that he was a noble who had eloped with a nun. He himself said he was a seigneur from near Lisle, who, having lost most of his fortune, had come to America in the hope of regaining it. He brought with him a charming young wife and two small children. After wandering aimlessly for some months and squandering most of his small capital in foolish land speculation, he was advised by the Chevalier de Goyen to go to an island in Oneida Lake. He sold his furniture, but not his library, and set out. Shortly after, he turned up at Oneida Lake, landed on his isolated island, unpacked his family silver and his truly fine library, and settled down as a farmer.[50]

Note Clarke's distinct separation of certainty and rumor. This is the way the Frenchman's story must be treated. The fact of his nobility remains, as does that of the romantic element his story has inspired. This romantic element's position in Lake Oneida history cannot be understated.

These romantic notions were manifested in literature in the early 1800's. A story, "Celeste: A Romance of Oneida Lake" appeared in the *Rome Sentinel* around this time. The author, J. M. T. Tucker, never became the O. Henry of his age, but his work does illustrate the

romantic feeling many people shared at this time about
Lake Oneida. The story is based on the life and adven-
tures of a Monsieur de Wardenou, third settler of the
town of Verona, near Sylvan Beach. Pomroy Jones cites
the story in his *Annals and Recollections of Oneida
County.*[51]

CELESTE: A ROMANCE OF ONEIDA LAKE
By J. M. T. Tucker

(Suggested by remarks of H. Baldwin, Esq., at
the Plank Road Celebration, Brewerton.)

Chapter I.

"They flee!
But see! Why turn they now to gaze,
Upon the gloomy, reddening sky?"

Early in the evening of a pleasant day in April, 1793,
might have been seen in a richly furnished parlor in
Havre, a young lady of moderate stature and moderate
personal attractions. A close examination, however, revealed a mind whose powers were developed in one of
the most intellectual pair of eyes ever placed beneath a
brow. These, although not the only token of intelligence,
never failed to impress the observer when they met his
own, with the superiority of their possessor. Connected
with these were strong developments of benevolence, and
of a noble and generous heart. She was being loved for
herself — for her amiable qualities, by one whose mind
was not enslaved by sensual passions.

As we introduce her, she was sitting by a window,
apparently waiting the arrival of some one. She leaves
the window and proceeds to her room, and presently returns to receive the message for her father — requiring
her to prepare for a journey to London in twenty-four

hours. With a pale and agitated countenance, and with a trembling hand, she endorsed the message —

"I will be ready to depart."
Celeste"

Handing it to the servant, she orders him to retire, and again takes her place weeping at the window.

The clock struck the hour of twelve. All was still in the mansion of the rich merchant La Fargo. A dull taper was burning in the room of Celeste, which revealed equippage for a journey in readiness, and a male servant armed and in disguise. The lady was still at the window. A carriage appeared at a distance in the street leading from the mansion. Presently, one of the windows are closed as if by accident. Instantly, with a still and cautious tread, the lady leaves the window, and in a moment is moving toward the street from a rear entrance. The carriage is muffled — the watch allow it to pass at a signal from its occupant, and turn away smiling, as the shining metal dazzles in the lamp-light upon their palms, whispering as they meet:

"Fine fellow that, fine operation, b'gar."

The lady is in the carriage, and soon all is still again in that mansion and in the streets.

It is morning soon, and a couple habited as travelers, with baggage, with male and female servants, appearing to be of middle age, descended from a hotel, and repair to a ship, bound for the United States. The wind is fair, and soon they are under way.

Great excitement prevails in the mansion of La Fargo! The hour of breakfast has come, and the summons does not bring down the beloved daughter. A servant is dispatched — the father turns lest she is sick, and will be unable to perform the journey — perhaps she has destroyed herself! No, she is too sensible for that, perhaps—

"Speak girl, why does not your mistress come to breakfast?"

"Not there! Here is a letter I found addressed to your honor."

Havre, 1793, 12 midnight

Dear Father: — I am sorry to leave you — but regard the separation your departure to England would create between myself and him who has long occupied the strongest affections of my heart, a great affliction. As a father you have my love — will ever have it. As a husband La Nouresse has my heart — must control it. Be not alarmed. Ere breakfast passes tomorrow, I shall be on my way to America — from which place you shall hear from me.

"Affectionately, farewell,"
"Celeste"

"Gone to America! Marry La Nouresse! Never! My carriage! My pistols! Ho, there, DeNair! Quick, you blockhead!"

"DeNair has gone, too, master, and broken the heart of his poor mother."

"To the ship then — let us away — police!"

"O, the ship has gone — been gone two hours!"

Chapter II.

Four years had elapsed. A gentleman and a lady were seen walking along the beach of one of the sweetest little lakes in the State of New York, called Oneida. A convenient log house, not splendid like a city mansion, but comfortable, stood a little distance from the shore. The forest around them was echoing with the sound of the axe and the falling trees. Out of the bosom of the lake danced the canoe, as the waves sped before the wind.

Here and there in the distance around them inland, the smoke curled as it arose and parted upon the air, showing that they were not altogether alone. Were they happy? Listen.

Said LaNouresse, as he fixed his soft expressive eyes upon Celeste:

"Four years have now passed away since we left our home in France, tell me love, are you happy — do you regret our adventure?"

"I have but one answer to give, and as they say, the truest language of the heart is expressed in song, I will answer you." Then in a voice as melodious and distinct as the harp she sang:

"Let others seek, in wealth or fame,
    A splendid path whereon to tread;
I'd rather wear a lowlier name,
    With loves' enchantment round it shed.
Fame's but alight to gild the grave,
    And wealth can never calm the breast;
But love, a halycon on life's wave,
    Hath power to soothe its strifes to rest."

"And have you no wish to exchange our rude dwelling and these wild scenes, for the gaiety or retirement of our native city?"

"Oh! not the smiles of other lands,
    Though far and wide our feet may roam,
Can e'er untie the genial bands
    That knit our hearts to home."

Again Celeste sang in the same sweet voice — but added — "Still I am happier here," as she gently leaned her head upon the breast of her husband.

La Nouresse felt the blood rush to his face, as his heart vibrated to the magic power of that love which had transplanted the angelic being from the soil of her birth and culture-surrounded by all the advantages of wealth and distinction, into a foreign clime, and upon a wilderness soil, subject to deprivation and many hardships. And when he reflected that, in flying from home and a father's stern command, to escape the doom of a union with a nobleman, because she loved an untitled, unwealthy merchant, he was proud of his seclusion. That being was a treasure, which titles and wealth could not estimate.

Once Celeste had written to her father. She had painted the scenes in which she moved, with all the poetry and romance of life. She represented her situation with that enthusiasm which it inspired in her own heart. She made her home in the "American wilderness," a transcript of Eden before the expulsion.

To that letter an answer was sent full of bitter unforgiveness. It was a severe blow to the gentle heart of a daughter. But she reasoned correctly, that, as to the choice of her life's companion, if she had made that life a delight, the complaints of her father, however well designed, were unreasonable — filial love cannot ask the sacrifice of a life to the pleasure of another's will. Life is our own — its happiness our own.

Chapter III.

Another four years had passed away. It was late at evening. The gentle breath of spring, perfumed by the fragrant wild flowers that adorned the luxuriant openings, and that crept to the very threshold of the happy cottage, was moving across the bosom of the lake and wildly murmuring in ripples along the shore, while the voice of the night bird was heard in echoes among the forest hills. Upon the floor of the cottage danced a bright-eyed little boy, whom his mother in her forgiving love named La Fargo, after his unforgiving grandfather, and upon the grass plot in front of the dwelling in many gambols frolicked the dogs, who had not yet retired and with all, it was a happy scene.

A coach is seen far away down the road, leading from the Mohawk turnpike, and running for many miles upon the lake shore. Nearer it approaches, until near the house of LaNouresse it stopped and the driver called out:

"Can you direct us to the residence of a gentleman whose name is La Nouresse, anywhere in these parts!"

"I have the honor to be that person," was the reply.

In a moment the coach stood before the door. A gentleman alighted. He was apparently about fifty-five years of age, richly dressed, and wealthy. The darkness obscured his face, and he was not recognized by the owner of the dwelling, who politely invited him to walk in, while himself directed in securing the beasts.

A shriek from his wife soon called LaNouresse into this house again.

On entering the door he saw the stranger prostrate upon the floor, and his wife in a swoon by his side. The man was dead! He had discovered himself to his long absent daughter, and being overcome by the intenseness of his feelings, fell at her feet, uttering the first and the last, the only words — "Daughter!" "Forgive!"

Deep was the affliction of that little family that night. Long and tenderly with tears sat Celeste by the cold form of her father. That sweet word "daughter," and the sweeter word "forgive," were oft pronounced amid the disturbed slumbers of the night.

The last tribute of respect had been paid to the departed father. Upon examining his papers, a will, prepared previously to his departure from France, was found duly attested, making Celeste the heir of one million francs and all his estates at Havre.

Besides this, among his papers addressed to his daughter, which he had prepared previously to leaving, and during his voyage, to provide against sudden death, was a full expression of his entire approbation of the marriage of Celeste to La Nouresse, and an account of the great injury done him by the nobleman who had won his confidence, and through whose influence he had, by misguided ambition, been induced to attempt her compulsory union with a villain, instead of being united to the worthy person of her heart's first choice.

Five years more had passed. La Nouresse had disposed of his property in America, and was among the wealthiest, most respected merchants in Havre.

One of his daughters is the happy wife of an American merchant — a son of a New England mechanic who resided in New York. That merchant, with his lady, visited the shores of the beautiful lake this summer.

Such are life's changes and romances.

Fini

The actual story is far less romantic. De Wardenou and "Celeste" emigrated to the United States to escape a ban on their marriage. He had a considerable fortune, which he invested and lost. The couple then moved to Lake Oneida, where a child was born. The child died, at an early age, in 1797.[52]

It is easy to laugh at the blustering, awkward writing style of J. M. T. Tucker, but his writing has its place in Lake Oneida's history. The story communicates to us an aesthetic idea about the lake. Phrases like "sweetest little lake," "wildly murmuring ripples along the shore," and "a transcript of Eden before the expulsion" contribute to building an idea that Lake Oneida and its country were a sort of "other Eden," a paradise and refuge for the romantic. The lake, said many, was beautiful. Its environs complemented it. Tucker grasped the reality of Oneida's aesthetics.

Alexis de Tocqueville, author of *Democracy in America,* recorded his romantic impressions of Lake Oneida and its sphere. De Tocqueville actually lived his words as he wrote:

A solemn silence reigned in this profound solitude. Scarcely a living creature was to be seen. Man was absent, and yet it was not a desert. On the contrary, nature exhibited a productive force unknown elsewhere. All was activity; the air appeared impregnated with an odor of vegetation; one seemed even to hear nature at work, and to see sap and life circulating through the ever open channels.

. . . Lake Oneida stands in the midst of low hills, and of still virgin forests. A belt of thick foliage surrounds it on every side; its waters bathe the roots of the trees, which are reflected on its calm, transparent face; a single fisherman's cabin is the only dwelling on its shore. Not a sail was to be seen on its whole expanse, nor even smoke ascending from the woods.[53]

De Tocqueville was enamoured by Lake Oneida, with the romance that surrounded it and with the Frenchman's story. The solitude and majesty of life on the lake inspired him to these words:

"The only happiness in this world is on the Lake Oneida.[54]

Lake Oneida, the early years. Many people experienced the region in those years. There were those who lived first, the Iroquois. But they, as was the case with all American Indians, were replaced in a sad, ignominious conquest by the white man.

The white man came to Oneida: the French warrior

Champlain, the Jesuit Bruyas, the English and French armies battling for regional domination, the Dutch scholar Van Der Kemp, the dreaming, calculating Clinton and Watson, the worldly Rochefaucault, the romantic DeTocqueville, the travellers to the great west and those who envisioned the magnificence of Lake Oneida and America.

Lake Oneida occupied a significant geographical position in those years. This was a main route across America. People had to come this way. People had to travel and to see, hear, feel the Lake Oneida region.

A superb location the lake had. Its aesthetic qualities were also beyond question. The eternal virgin forests. The placid broad water. The salmon. The endless cream beaches along which the pen of Tucker strolled. It was, and is, not difficult for the romantic to dwell in blissful dreams here.

This location and this "other Eden." When the time came for upstaters to think of their pleasures and of the idea of "resort" they thought of the Lake Oneida.

And of Sylvan Beach.

BEGINNINGS

On the east of the Lake Oneida there is a
beautiful shelving beach . . . the north
shore is remarkable for its bold and picturesque beauty.

—J. Disturnell
The Picturesque Tourist, 1858

Sylvan Beach, Township of Vienna, Oneida County, New York. Throughout its history, Vienna has been a lightly populated, agrarian town"ship. Its principal villages, aside from Sylvan Beach, are named Fish Creek Landing, Jewell, McConnellsville, North Bay, and Vienna. Individually owned businesses and industry are the rule here. At one time the township could boast thirty-seven sawmills, but all were small, private enterprises. [1] Nineteenth century North Bay's economy centered, for a large part, on boat building, mainly canalboats, but the industry never employed enough people to effect any degree of urbanization on the settlement.

Vienna native pronounce the town's name "Vieenna." George Scriba's original name for the land that encompassed Vienna Township was "Embden." Vienna was created from Camden township on April 3, 1807, the title "Orange" being then bestowed on it. The year 1808 witnessed a name changing from Orange to "Bengal." Reports tell us that panthers were known in the town at that time. Finally, in April of 1816, Vienna became Vienna. [2] The town encompasses townships nine and ten of the old Scriba Patent. Sandy soil prevails, with fertile alluvial fields gracing the Fish Creek flood plain area.

A drive through Vienna brings one close to rural America, this country's heartland. Proportioned, white church spires identify the villages and hamlets. Farm children ride up and down one-laned country roads that occasionally serve two autos at once. These roads have character, twisting, bumping their textured way through the township. Some even are bordered by rows of great pines, forming medieval walkways with escape only to the sky. The pines date from CCC times, when the government was able sustenance for Vienna, and most of this nation.

Several amusing hunting tales decorate early Vienna township history. Pomroy Jones, creator of *Annals and Recollections of Oneida County,* narrates one story about a hapless French hunter.

> In 1800, a Frenchman, from New York, came to this town on a hunting expedition. He was possessed of the two most necessary articles to the hunter, a valuable dog and a good gun. He stopped at Barnard's Bay (north shore of Oneida Lake) and his first essay was in hunting deer. He went into the woods, and had not proceeded far before his dog discovered, what Mons. Crapeau supposed to be, a fine deer in a tree top. He shot at the animal, wounding, but not disabling it. It leaped from the tree, and on reaching the ground, was grappled by the dog. A furious fight ensued, but the dog was however soon put 'hors du combat,' when our hunter thought it time to interfere to save the life of his favorite. He had nothing but his unloaded gun and valuable as it was, it did not come in competition with the life of the hound. The first blow broke it in two at the breech, without in the least stunning the doubly infuriated animal, now disposed to make fight with both master and dog. Our hero nought intimidated, and having a good club in the breechless gun barrel, gave a lucky blow which broke the 'critter's back.'[3]

That "deer" was pure hellfired panther — it gave birth to no fawns. Rochefaucault told how the French in

America disliked Americans. Judging from this tale, it seems that some Americans held a rather uncomplimentary view of the citified French.

Vienna experienced a wolf problem around 1820. Wolves, present in numbers "as thick as blackbirds," terrorized the town's livestock.[4] Determined to remedy the situation, the town's male residents, five hundred in number, banded together and organized a massive wolf hunt. North Bay was the scene. The men formed a huge, sweeping semicircle and pushed their way forward to the shores of Lake Oneida, forcing all terrestial wildlife to flee before their advancing heels. When the beach was reached, the slaughter began! Three wolves and over fifty rabbits lost their lives in this epic safari of Vienna township history.[5]

North Bay, located on Lake Oneida's northeast corner, has a short, but interesting history as a nineteenth century resort community. The town's resort status was most important in the last three decades of the century. Tourist accommodations of North Bay included the Tremont and Frisbie Houses, the Butler and the North Bay Hotel, the latter being in tavern use to this day. Primary customers at these hotels were sportsmen, fishermen and, of course, hunters who visited Lake Oneida and the Vienna woods.

Vienna was and is a country township. Verona, the township due south of Vienna, is of a similar character. The first settler in Sylvan Beach's immediate area, according to most Oneida County historians, came to Verona from Berkshire County, Massachusetts, in May of 1796.[6] His name was Asahel Jackson. He and his family settled near the then abandoned Royal Blockhouse, across river from contemporary Sylvan Beach.

Asahel established a public house for the accommodation of the many travelers and boatmen who journeyed through the water highway at his doorstep. DeWitt

Clinton mentions his stay at the Jackson Tavern in his diary. Clinton was examining possible routes for the Erie Canal during his trip.

At Jackson's death, his wife assumed proprietorship of the tavern. Mrs. Jackson was reported to be a fine innkeeper and, above all, a tough woman of the frontier. Christian Schultz, a German traveler in America (1807-1808), met Mrs. Jackson and recorded his impressions.

> There is a tolerably good tavern kept at this place by a Mrs. J. . . and her sister, a young woman, who, you may be assured, display no ordinary degree of courage in dealing out whiskey to thirty or forty Indians, who generally rendezvous at this place, especially as there is no other white settler within sight or call . . .[7]

In 1825 the Erie Canal opened, excluding the Lake Oneida water route. Few people now passed down Wood Creek, across the lake. Mrs. Jackson was forced to close her tavern doors and move.

The completion of the Erie Canal in 1825 greatly diminished travel and trade through the Lake Oneida thoroughfare.[8] The lake's position as a central waterway in New York State was not lost for long, however, as the Oneida Lake Canal Company was formed in 1832 with the expressed purpose of utilizing the easily navigated, lengthy Oneida.[9] New York State authorized the company to establish and run the Oneida Lake Canal for fifty years, charging tolls which were not to exceed those of the Erie. On September 12, 1835, the canal was finished.[10] It flowed from a point on the Erie at Higginsville to the approximate intersection of Wood and Fish Creeks, a total length of about six and one-half miles. The canal had one guard and seven lift locks and a fall of fifty-seven and one-half feet, at low water on the lake. Its width and depth were basically the same as those of the Erie. The final completion costs for the canal were $78,829. Total revenues for the canal, during its entire history, amounted to $65,839.[11] Adding improvement and toll-collecting costs to the original construction expense makes one realize the losing nature of this canal enterprise.

Ulysses Prentiss Hedrick's history of New York agriculture contains explanation of the first Oneida Lake Canal's importance. In describing the specifics of the canal, Mr. Hedrick writes:

> The Oneida Lake Canal was an important link in the waterway system of the State, since it afforded navigation from the Erie to Oneida Lake and by the Oneida outlet (at Brewerton) to the Oswego Canal and river. Before the Erie was built, the Oneida Lake route was the great thoroughfare for water transportation of goods westward, and many of the settlers in western New York came through these waters.[12]

This canal was extremely important to the previously cited boatbuilders of North Bay as it gave them an easy outlet to the Erie and, thus, their markets.

A second Oneida Lake Canal was built in 1877, at a cost of over four hundred thousand dollars.[13] This canal provided water access from the Erie at Durhamville to Upper South Bay on the lake. The five and three tenths mile long canal was never a success and was abandoned in 1887.[14] Both the Lake Oneida canals are still in existence and can be seen, though upstate's human and natural civilization are rapidly eroding their identity.

Aesthetical and empirical appreciation of the Lake Oneida continued throughout the nineteenth century. Christian Schultz, that acquaintance of the Jackson women, wrote of the lake:

> Oneida Lake is a most charming and beautiful

sheet of water, about thirty miles in length and
five in breadth, and, I believe, affords the best and
greatest variety of fish of any water in the western
part of this state.[10]

A "charming and beautiful sheet of water." Schultz recorded that he encountered an Oneida Indian with his
prize catch, a thirty pound salmon. Schultz was impressed, unknowingly linking himself with those who saw
great potential in the Lake Oneida.

Gazeteers of the century echoed founded sentiments
about Lake Oneida. Bishop Davenport, author of *Davenport's Gazeteer* (1836), mentioned the lake, saying
"Oneida Lake receives Wood Creek on the East end, and
communicates with Lake Ontario by the Oswego. It is a
most beautiful lake abounding in fish." Darby and
Dwight's *New Gazetteer of the United States* (1833) cited
the lake with the words, "This lake being the important
channel of intercourse between the Canadians and the
five nations of Indians, up to the time of the French
wars . . . the banks are low, with good soil . . ." Then
there was John Disturnell's *The Picturesque Tourist*
(1858). Disturnell did more than describe when he wrote,
"On the east of the Lake Oneida there is a beautiful shelving beach . . . the north shore is remarkable for its bold
and picturesque beauty." That "shelving beach" —
people would soon call it "sylvan."

Even the county historian got into the act of Lake
Oneida adoration. Samuel Durant's Oneida County history (1878) mentions Oneida's virtues in its Vienna
township section. The historian's tangent reads:

> Oneida Lake, viewed from any point in this
> town, is a beautiful sheet of water . . . The view
> from the promontory at North Bay, when a fresh
> wind is blowing and the sky is clear or partly
> cloudy, is one long remembered. Stretching away

> to the west and south, the blue waters of the lake
> appear magnificent with their curling waves and
> caps of foam, and on the opposite shore the dis-
> tant hills of Madison County rise bold and free
> — a fitting background for an exquisite picture.[16]

This historian finds the adjectives "bold and free" to be
particularly fitting. The Lake Oneida is that way — no
one can harness her, though there were many who tried.
The lake is a magnificent stallion galloping across the
great plains. Other times she is the lover, quiet and serene,
caressing in the movement of her ripples. Only one thing
is certain about her nature — she is good to those who
know and respect her.

Lake Oneida has had its "seers' 'and its "doers." The
former leave their words, hopefully their images. The
latter leave a mark, a physical one. Like Scriba. And
James D. Spencer.

Verona, like Vienna, grew slowly. James D. Spencer
came to the town from West Monroe, New York, in the
early 1840's.[17] The move was not a momentous one, as
West Monroe is on Lake Oneida's northwest shores.
James was born on December 27, 1813, in Amsterdam,
New York.[18] His mother died when he was thirteen and
the family settled in West Monroe. At the age of fifteen
he became clerk of a general store.

In Verona, James resided in the hamlet of Fish
Creek, about a mile east of the Royal Blockhouse site.
During his eighty-six living years he had three wives,
Freelove Raymond, Elizabeth Fisher, and Mrs. Margaret
Williams. Freelove and James begat three sons, Reuben,
Houghton, and Lyman, and a daughter, Millie, who died
at age thirty. Elizabeth bore him Catherine, deceased at
age four, and Bruce Lamott. Margaret and James were
wed late in life.

Daniel Wager, a member of that small, select group of Oneida County historians, lauded James Spencer with the words:

> He began life virtually an orphan boy, and through industry and good judgment has secured a competency.[19]

Industry. Good judgment. Those qualities James Spencer most certainly had. James engaged in farming, in the sand business, ran a tavern, and in 1847 began a series of Verona and Vienna real estate investments. These speculations led to the genesis of Sylvan Beach.

From 1847 to 1877, James acquired over four hundred acres of land in Verona and over two hundred-sixty in Vienna.[20] The latter parcels were located in present-day Sylvan Beach; the Verona land encompassed the northwestern portion of the township, near Lake Oneida and Wood Creek. Spencer invested over twelve thousand dollars in the land and also paid for its clearing by the firm of Hoyt, Littlejohn and Hoyt. His returns on the investment would not be substantial until the 1880's.

Spencer's sons, Reuben and Lyman, assisted him in the real estate business. Reuben, especially, was instrumental to the business's success. Wager said of him, "He assists his father in superintending and developing the same (real estate) at Sylvan Beach and vicinity."[21] In 1873, Reuben, Lyman and their wives, Amy and Mary, concluded lease negotiations that resulted in the construction of Sylvan Beach's first resort facility.[22] Amy and Mary were co-signers of the lease. Sewell Newhouse, representative of the Oneida community, was the other party in the deal. This Community was an experiment in utopian living, begun by John Humphrey Noyes at Sherrill, New York. Newhouse invented a specialized animal trap, the manufacture of which provided a basis for much

VIENNA TOWNSHIP PICTORIALS
ONEIDA COUNTY
NEW YORK

Resident, Route 49, near Vienna hamlet

A Farm, Fish Creek Flood Plain Area, Summer and Winter

A boy bicycling, Cook Road

A township cemetery overlooking the lake.

Farmer in his fields, Vienna Township
. . . a country township

James D. Spencer, founder of Sylvan Beach

River front still life at the Algonquin Hotel, 1884-85. (Courtesy Ed Stewart)

Spencer's Forest Home, built in 1879 — from a later photo.

Sylvan Beach Union Chapel, built on land donated by the Spencers. 1887.
The chapel was featured in the film, "The Sterile Cuckoo.'

First bridge over the Wood River — this amazingly clear photo shows the fine detail of this bridge, which replaced privately-operated ferry boats.
(Courtesy Glenn Chesebrough)

O & W Railroad bridge over Barge Canal, Fish Creek Hamlet

STODDARD & GARVIN.

BEACON BEACH
FISH CREEK
WOOD RIVER
SYLVAN BEACH

ADDRESS ONEIDA NY
UNTIL JUNE 1 ST

FISH CREEK P.O. N.Y.

A portion of Algonquin Hotel poster, showing Main Street in its frontier glory and several early names for the Beach.

In addition to their real estate ventures, the Spencers operated this tavern and the Forest Home in Sylvan Beach's beginning years.

(Courtesy Ed Stewart)

of the Community's economy. He was one of the Community's business representatives.

The lease was designed for ninety-nine years, at the paltry sum of twenty-five dollars per year.[23] The Oneida Community sought a resort cottage near their Sherrill home and, as they fished Lake Oneida and could ride the Oswego-Midland Railway to a point one mile from the cottage's site, they chose to build there.

The aesthetics of Lake Oneida inspired the romantic element of the Oneida Community. *The Circular,* the Community's newspaper, a "weekly journal of home, science, and general intelligence," contained expression of Community feeling for the lake.

> We returned to the cottage contented with our luck, and enjoyed the picturesqueness and grandeur of the scenery around us. The lake was now smooth as glass, the sky unclouded; the sunset had faded away leaving a faint streak of yellow light on the western horizon; the air was ringing with the voices of insects; frogs were humming, birds were singing their evening songs, and loud above all was the continuous note of the whip-poor-will.[24]

Community people thought it altogether fitting and proper to name their cottage. The story of the process through which they arrived at a name provides us with a very humorous photo of the history of Sylvan Beach.

> A name being wanted for the lodge at the Lake, a paper was put on the bulletin-board, whereon persons were requested to record their preference. The three names that got the most votes were, Lake House, Bleak House, and Lodge. Many others such as Down There, Khan, Lake Side, Retreat, Cottage by the Sea, etc., were suggested.

One individual, who had come from a two-day's sojourn at the place and whose experiences of wind, snow-storms, freezing streams and railroad perils were somewhat startling to his homegoing imagination, proposed to call it "The Jaws of Death." After an amusing discussion one evening the popular vote finally hit on "Joppa" as the most satisfactory.[25]

"The Jaws of Death." It takes but little imagination to realize how amusing that discussion must have been.

"Joppa" held significance to the Community people. This significance was explained by *The Circular*.

> . . . Joppa was suggested. We like this name because it was short, unique and scriptural; and no sooner had she appropriated it than Augusta found from the books that the word Joppa signifies comely, pleasant, so that it seems we had unwittingly made another good hit. A reference to Robinson's Calmet gives the following items of interest concerning Joppa: "Joppa, lying on the southeastern Mediterranean coast, is one of the most ancient seaports in the world . . ."[26]

"Joppa" was often used by non-Community persons to refer to the area of Sylvan Beach, thus making it our second pre-"Sylvan Beach" area title. With the disbanding of the Community around 1880 Joppa, as a resort facility, ceased to exist.

Myths of buried treasure spice the history of many cities, regions and lakes. Sylvan Beach has its treasure myth and it goes like this:

> About 1870, a stock company was formed to discover, if possible, cannon which was supposed to be buried around there (junction of Fish and

Wood Creeks), filled with gold and silver. After digging to some depth they struck something, they knew not what, but before they could ascertain, the horses (that furnished the power) gave out and before they could replenish same, the place they had excavated filled up with water and probabilities are if there is any treasure buried in this vicinity, it will never be discovered.[27]

It was never discovered and, like all good myths, the cannon legend remains in imagination and dream. The gold and silver of Sylvan Beach was not resting in cannon.

The Spencers discovered the truth in those words.

1879. Lyman C. Spencer builds the first public house in Sylvan Beach.[28] He names it the "Forest Home." His hotel is equipped with boat house, dock, bath-house, an excellent restaurant, and access to five miles of the finest bathing beach in the world. Lyman secures rights to operate a ferry across Wood Creek, carrying people from Verona to Vienna. Trains deliver tourists to the Fish Creek Station, whereupon they embark by foot or boat to Lake Oneida. The Forest Home stands and is in operation today, oldest resort facility in Sylvan Beach.

James D. Spencer was the sole real estate developer in Sylvan Beach at this time. These years, 1873 to 1891, saw the beginnings of Lake Oneida's most prominent resort. The actual date of the village's first major growth can be determined by recording the number of Spencer's property sales, year by year. When this is completed, the information reads as follows:

1873 to 1880	7 sales	1885	18
1881	13	1886	22
1882	19	1887	10
1883	11	1888	7
1884	19	1889 to 1891	14

The numbers include sales recorded in Reuben's name, as well as that of James.[29] It was a family enterprise.

When a town has but one real estate man, that town's growth is directly related to that man's sales. Spencer's dealings show us that the first real growth of Sylvan Beach can be dated around 1881, two years after the Forest Home's founding. Daniel Wager reinforces this conclusion in his Oneida County history. He refers to the fact that Sylvan Beach, a "noted summer resort," had gained reputation in the past fifteen years. Wager's history was copyrighted in 1896.[30]

*　*　*　*　*

ROME SENTINEL . . . July 19, 1881 . . . Steamers on Oneida Lake run in connection with Midland trains daily from the railroad bridge at Fish Creek, to convey pleasure parties to any point on the lake. All trains stop at the landing.

*　*　*　*　*

1881: the year of Sylvan Beach's initial genesis.

An interesting community was born then, in a most pastoral setting. There was no sense of structured settlement identity there. It was just a "place" on Oneida's east shore. But, oh what a place!

It didn't know what to call itself.

"Joppa" was far gone by now, passed by as utopian ideals evaporated in upstate's hostile clime. Some persons resorted to geography in naming the settlement, using the placenames "Wood River" and "Fish Creek" (also the name of the local train station). These geographical labels were temporal, however. Around the middle of August, 1881, "Sylvan Beach" received a semipermanent identity. Newspapers reported:

The Utica Herald says: 'People of good taste who live in the vicinity of that portion of Oneida

Lake now called Fish Creek propose to change the name to Beacon Beach, a pretty substitute. It is a historical tradition that one of the two old trees used by the Indians and traders as a landmark in navigating the lake yet remains standing.[31]

But this "Beacon Beach" brand didn't suit all, either. The Rome Sentinel employed a "Sylvan Beach" correspondent back then to cover the resort's early growth. He cringed in sardonic prose at the thought of "Beacon Beach."

> Some aesthetically inclined people, I hear, have christened this locality Beacon Beach. I much prefer the time-honored appellation, 'Spencer's.' (Spencer Beach is a variation on that, also used in the early 1880's.)[32]

The man called himself "Cosmost,' leaguing himself in pseudonym with the rampant 19th century upstate classicism revival.

Cosmos' writings delve into the trivial, factual and flippantly philosophical aspects of the Sylvan Beach naissance. If one could travel through time and ask the man the question, "My friend, tell me, what is going on out there at Landlord Spencer's balliwyk, he might reply in like manner. [33]

> FOREST HOME, FISH CREEK, AUGUST 10, 1881: Although not on guard duty, I feel rather Sentinelly (don't get it sentimentally) and will proceed to gather up the fragments that nothing may be lost.

> This is a most attractive locality, this product of Landlord Spencer's industry and sweat, in which the writer finds "retreat," as opposed to "resort." There is nothing here of the hustle, the maddening throngs that populate our other relaxation locales. An absence of the frivolous requirements of fashion even prevails here. Mr.

Spencer, by the way, seems to understand what so few landlords do, that summer boarders desire nothing generally, so much as good, plain, substantial fare and plenty of letting alone. A walk in the towering grove. A lovers' stroll in the sand. The fisherman bobs for his wary quarry. A fatigued Roman finds retreat at Spencer's.

The other morning I strolled past the barn and observe an ax grinding in progress. I stopped to study the operation. The holder of the ax was ye hostler of this institution and the man at the crank was one of his campers. The weather was warm, the ax dull, the hostler bore on heavily, maliciously I thought, from the twinkle of his eye, and ye noble Roman perspired fearfully; yet he also persevered, as a Roman should, and when his task was finished ye ax was sharp. From all I could learn this was a labor of love — a casting of bread upon the waters. The scene has vanished, but the picture remains.

A Mr. J. S. Cottman, also of Roman birth, sits under his own vine and fig tree, smoking his pipe in temporary oblivion to the duties of busy life. Below his feet, the Wood River flows, feeding the constant thirst of the broad Oneida.

Fish stories are in order, but none have thus far turned up which were not backed by the fish. Why is it that fishing develops in a man an almost uncontrollable propensity to fib? It requires very little ingenuity to create a six-pound pike from a veteran sucker; but when a man catches a dozen small fish and says many of them would weigh a pound, is he not guilty of an attempt at misleading the public mind?

But I am getting prolix, and so, leaving moonlight walks and midnight sails, and other things more or less interesting to those who love to dwell thereon, I am . . . Cosmos.

The pastoral life on Oneida: it was, undoubtedly,

more difficult and harsh than this, but it had, as it did throughout history, the ability to inspire. Only now things were different. Men, the Spencers, were working from the inspiration, to build and develop a retreat.

Retreats are, of definition and necessity, small enclaves. Sylvan Beach, in the mid 1880's, began a definite move away from the Cosmos ideal, toward the "resort" image.

Sylvan Beach's first large resort facility was the Algonquin Hotel, built in 1884 by C. G. W. Stoddard and Anthony T. Garvin of Oneida, New York. In the words of the proprietors, the Algonquin was:

> ... an elegant, new summer hotel, just finished and furnished with every regard for comfort. A first class restaurant (is) connected with the house, open at all hours, with a splendid bill of fare.[34]

The "Great Refrigerator" of the Algonquin holds five hundred tons of ice. The hotel's river front dock is three hundred feet long! Hickory groves along the lake are owned by the hotel and available, along with that indescribably sandy beach, for the use of all guests. The scene unfolds as . . .

> Upstream you see the encottaged banks, the mingled yellow and green of willow fringe and hickory thicket along the shore, the quaint ferry above, the widesweeping, silent stream, so like that flood of Tennyson's, down which floated fair Elaine to the imploring Launcelot.[35]

They called the town a "summer city in the wilderness." Steamers ran up river to meet trains at the Fish Creek station. Many people preferred the easy, green walk from station to resort. Sylvan Beach felt growth pains, echoed by the Algonquin's brochure.

Rounding the sunny side bend (of Wood
River), the full life of this new river town bursts
upon him (the traveler). The picturesque cottages
hang upon the banks or look out brightly from the
hickory copses along the stream. The river is alive
with pleasure boats . . . the scene is restful as well
as active; there is diversion — quiet interest —
healing for tired brains — in the bobbing of the
boats . . . in the liquid clamor of propellors, in all
the 'quiet noise' about you.[36]

Other hotels sprouted in mid-1880's Sylvan Beach.
Franklin Stevens operated the "Lake Beach Hotel" and
donated land to the railroad to build a passenger line into
Sylvan Beach. "Gorm" Armstrong, of Rome, kept the
Oneida Lake House. Landlord Spencer's Forest Home
was thriving. Cafes, stores, more and more cottages filled
the landscape. There was even a laundry service and a
photographer peddled his tin type magic. A small carnival area became popular, with a fat-ladied museum,
games galore, and the roller coaster. Of the latter, it was
said:

The song of the roller coaster again entices,
and there is the same, frantic, blissful 'utterness'
in its swoop as of yore.[37]

Peace, bliss, harmony and all were not the rule in
early Sylvan Beach. In June of 1887 a dispute arose
among ferry operators over rights to the Wood River
crossings. Money, root of all evil to some, started the
controversy. The Rome Sentinel narrated the story of
the Sylvan Beach ferry war. Follow it with patience,
and be open to interpretation.

A war of great importance has been pending
for some time among the ferry forces. The horse
ferry is rented to C. Clifford, who runs it at the

same old rates for teams. L. C. Spencer ran his little ferry at five cents a head. Some picnics (large train excursions to Sylvan Beach) are advertised to come here on the E.C. & N. making their headquarters at the Algonquin. Charles Stoddard, the proprietor of the Algonquin, thought it would be a handsome compliment to pay them in return to arrange for their transportation across the stream to and fro, free, and hired his boats and men for the purpose. When this bomb burst it shook things here worse than any Anarchist explosion ever shook Chicago. Result: Houghton Spencer and the Algonquin will each run ferries for low rates; therefore, Spencer & Randall must or get no custom.[38]

The Elmira, Cortland and Northern railroad line (E.C. & N.—Lehigh Valley) ended across Wood River, at Verona Beach. There was no river bridge at the time and ferries had to do for the non-swimming tourist. The Algonquin's owners got their way in this dispute and that is an important item to note. This was the big hotel in town. It was a prime drawing card — it included more rooms than all the other hotels combined. This amounted to power within the community, power that Stoddard and Garvin were not loathe to flex when the issue was financial gain.

Back to the lighter side of things. What follows is an 1886 saga of "A Game Constable's Shrewd Scheme to Capture (Poachers') Nets." Fish pirates have always thrived on Lake Oneida — the lake is a veritable garden of aquatic life, prime stuff for a cagy poacher.

The American Angler of May 15 contains the following correspondence from Oneida, signed 'Picus.' The wall-eyed pike have furnished heaps of sport in Fish Creek — more than for the past

ten years. The game constable has done his duty
for say the last three or five years, and now the
fishing shows an improvement. Seiners commenced operations again this spring as soon as
the ice was out, thinking that the game constable
was not awake, but the G.C. was on deck, and has
already brought in and burned thirty nets, valued
at $1500 to $2000. He caught twenty nets one day
last week in a very shrewd manner. He took one
good, plucky man with him and went in the night
to the northwestern shore of the lake, where by
secret advices, he knew there were seines in the
bay of the lake. The two men lay behind a wood
pile in the woods, getting all located before day-
break. Then by their orders the constable's steamboat came boldly across the lake to the bay with a
crew of plucky fellows. The seiners, who are always on the alert, saw the steamer coming for the
bay, when they up with the seines and hid them
within two hundred feet of the G.C. and companion who were behind the wood pile. When the crew
landed all joined and toted off to the steamer the
twenty seines, valued about $1200. The G.C., in
narrating the affair to me, said the atmosphere
was blue with curses, revolvers were shown, high
words, etc. On the fences all about were pickets
posted — women, boys, girls, tramps . . . [39]

"Picus." Could he have been a relation to our friend,
Cosmos? Only the Greeks would know.

Around May 8, 1886, Sylvan Beach received its official naming.[40] The Ontario and Western Railroad finished its "loop," which brought the road into Sylvan
Beach proper. A station grew up by the tracks. The company named the station "Sylvan Beach." The naming
was that simple.

This established a set name for the settlement, but did not lessen people's confusion with the resort's nomenclature. There were the lingering names Beacon Beach, Spencer's Beach, and now came the O. & W. with a new one — Sylvan Beach. What happened was an understandable upstate simplification. They called their village "The Beach." This ex officio jargon caught the ever-present vernacular and is used among upstaters to this day. People went to The Beach.

"Sylvan" derives its meaning from the latin "sylvanus," or "wooded." The word found application in an earlier Lake Oneida resort facility, the "Sylvan House," on Frenchman's Island. This hostel opened in August of 1851 and operated until its firey death on March 2, 1876. It was a prosperous establishment, attracting guests from as far away as New York (a $9 ride on the O. & W.)[41] The hostel's advertisement contained a pungent taste of Lake Oneida romanticism.

> Oneida Lake is one of the most beautiful of the inland lakes of New York, being 20 miles long and 6 wide. The fishing, boating, sailing and bathing are the best . . .
> When the Great Spirit formed the world, His smile rested on the waters of the blue Oneida, and Frenchman's Island arose to greet it.[42]

Perhaps railroad officials or someone within "The Beach" heard of the Sylvan House and found the name to their liking. Steamboats consistently ran from Sylvan Beach to Frenchman's. The connection is there but, sadly, it remains on the thin thread of speculation.

James D. Spencer first saw the gold on Oneida's east shore. During the 1880's, many others experienced latent visions of that prosperity. Recall that both the O. & W. and the E.C. & N. railroads extended lines into Sylvan Beach during this era. There was even talk of building a railroad from Rome to the lake. The Sentinel's "Man About Town" wrote of this speculation.

The building of a road from here to Oneida Lake has been talked of among Romans from time to time, but no action has ever been taken. There seems to be every prospect that Oneida Lake is to become the great central New York watering place. The importance which it has attained within the past five years is something remarkable. A proportionate advance in the next five years will fairly set the place booming. A railroad from Rome would help such a boom, and, at the same time, help Rome. This is a proposition that can be understood and appreciated by the dullest.[43]

A later issue of the Sentinel continued along a similar theme. The paper editorialized:

The excursion travel between Rome and the lake would be something enormous in the summer season, and those who have canvassed the matter think there is little doubt that the road would pay the year round. There are hundreds, if not thousands of people in Rome who never, or hardly ever, visit Oneida Lake because of the lack of transportation facilities. If they could board a train here in the morning and go to the lake for a day at a nominal expense they would go many times during the season.[44]

That last sentence is the key to understanding Sylvan Beach's boom and prosperous years. The railroads offered cheap, quick mass transportation to central New Yorkers. The workers, doctors, executives, housewives and chimney sweeps could afford to visit Sylvan Beach.

They could afford it. They came by the thousands. Even in the beginning resort years it was not uncommon to find three or four thousand picnickers at The Beach on a summer's day.

These were not all easy years, these early ones. The 1889 season could only be termed disastrous for the village's economy. The events of that year illustrate the effects of a great resort economy variable: the weather.

> A Roman who has spent some time at Sylvan Beach said: 'The resort has been very dull this summer. You see the season did not open very early (around July 10 — that's very late) and there have been a great many rainy days since it opened. The result has been light trade. I don't believe any man in business here has made anything this year. There have been days when there were not a dozen persons to be seen on the street or in the grove.[45]

That year's largest picnic, the Hop Growers' Association, was enveloped in deluge. This exemplified 1889. A lean year in a decade of relative plenty. By this early stage, however, Sylvan Beach was in a position where it could recover from a bad season. O. & W. railroad cars "packed with humanity" would come for years.

James D. Spencer was a benevolent, as well as ambitious man. As we shall later see, he donated land in 1887 for construction of Sylvan Beach's first church, the Union Chapel. Again, in 1890, Spencer exhibited his generous aspect, donating land between Railroad and Park Avenues for a huge, wooded village park. The Rome Sentinel described the park as it was first conceived.

> The park contains, according to the deed, 6.05 acres. Naturally the trees are its most valuable and interesting feature. Some of them are very old, possibly dating back to Shakespeare's time. Oaks predominate, but there are also maples and

pines. Numerous patches of white clover are in bloom during the season.

The park was not exactly a gift; it cost the "area" of Sylvan Beach the exorbitant sum of one dollar.

Spencer's deed for the park was contracted between himself, his wife and son, Reuben, and "Lyman Spencer, F. B. Randall and William H. Foster," trustees of the corporate "Public Park of Sylvan Beach." This gave the latter three the power of park administration. The deed stipulated specific qualifiers for park administration, however, qualifiers which, if not fulfilled, would necessitate the return of the park from village ownership to that of Spencer's heirs. Listen to James D. Spencer as he talks through these qualifiers — the words are those of a man concerned about a beautiful part of the town that he founded.

> ... that the said real estate (the park) shall be and forever remain a public park under the control of the trustees of said village (Sylvan Beach) and be devoted to the best interests of said village and the enjoyment, comfort and convenience of visitors and residents ...
>
> ... that the sale of wine, ale, beer and any and all malt, vicious and spiritous liquors on said premises and all species and kinds of gambling and gaming thereon shall be forever prohibited and further that in the event that said real estate shall be by the qualified electors of Sylvan Beach abandoned as such Public Park and cease to be used as such and in the event that said Trustees of Sylvan Beach shall knowingly and wilfully violate any of the above conditions against liquor selling and gambling, then the said real estate shall revert to and become the property of said parties of the first part (the Spencers), their heirs

and assigns forever, in all respects as though the conveyance had never been made.[42]

Spencer's ideas are clear. He wanted his park to remain as such, free of traditional vices and existing for the recreational "park" pleasures of the general public. "The park must remain a park," he might have declared. It was and should be an inviolate piece of green amidst humanity's see.

Beginnings . . . the birth of a resort village. Sylvan Beach emerges from agrarian townships, Vienna and Verona. It is small now. In just ten years it will rise to the position of the most prominent resort in central upstate New York. James D. Spencer was the man behind this ascendance. Spencer made the right moves. He bought and sold with success. In the American idyllic mold, Spencer earned the title of "poor boy made good." He and his family brought an area settled by two farmers (Adam Miller and the McClanathan brothers) and a group of utopians into resort status.

James D. Spencer died in 1899, at the age of eighty-six. In his later years he was indeed fortunate, being able to live and see "his" resort emerge into its golden age, the "Cavana Era."

THE CAVANA ERA

It is mostly through Dr. Cavana's efforts that Sylvan Beach is in a position where its future welfare cannot be gainsaid.

—*Souvenir, Attractions, and History of Sylvan Beach*, 1907

III

Thomas Carlyle, the historian, wrote:

As I take it, Universal History, the history of
what man has accomplished in this world, is at
bottom, the History of the Great Men who have
worked here. They were the leaders of men, these
great ones; the modellers, patterns, and in a wide
sense creators of whatsoever the general mass of
men contrived to do or to attain; all things that
we see standing accomplished in the world are
properly the outer material result, the practical
realisation and embodiment of thoughts that
dwelt in the Great Men sent into the world. The
soul of the whole world's history, it may justly be
considered, has been and is the history of these.[1]

Thus spoke Thomas Carlyle, historian of the nineteenth
century. Carlyle's interpretation of history, while it
raises question and leaves doubt, has something to it.
Great men, the hero figures, have come and gone. They
are remembered in books, in the American epic film, in
monuments, spiritual and physical alike, as having exerted a profound influence on their era. More often than
not, the degree of their charissma is exaggerated or romanticized. The fact of their influence remains, however,
and deserves treatment in the proper perspective.

Doctor Martin Cavana came to Sylvan Beach from
the city of Oneida, New York, in 1891.[2] In Oneida, Dr.
Cavana owned and operated a private hospital famous
for its "gold cure," a remedy for virtually any kind of
addiction. The doctor spent thirty-three years at Sylvan

Beach, residing there until his death in 1924. No man in the history of this resort community has exerted so great an impact on its being. Martin Cavana established a sanitarium and school for nurses on Park Avenue. Martin Cavana's promotional "chamber of commerce" activities brought fresh economy to Sylvan Beach. Martin Cavana gained control of the Midway, then known as Carnival Park, and expanded it. He held virtually every important public office, being President of the Sylvan Beach Corporation, the village's governing body, for many years. The name "Cavana" became synonymous with the success of Sylvan Beach, and with the disappointment. "The Coney Island of Central New York" clothed the idea of "Sylvan Beach" during the Cavana Era. For people who experienced those words, Sylvan Beach found few aesthetic or amusement equals in the world. Upstate, after all, was their world and in upstate there was only one Sylvan Beach.

The Cavana Era fascinates me more than any other time in this community's history in that the era was as much an "ideal" as it was a reality. Remember what Carlyle said: "they (the great men) were . . . in a wide sense creators of whatsoever the general mass of men contrived to do or attain." Martin Cavana was the model for Sylvan Beach, the generator of optimism and good feeling for his child. He and his tireless effort on the village's behalf created a prosperity ideal. Not that success was absent, but even in the rough years the Cavana spirit brought confidence in recovery, in a good year to come, a better day tomorrow. The man reached into his pocket to help businesses in need. He opened his kitchen to insure that families "without" had enough to eat. He and his friends kept a grand, glittering hotel open to generate inspiration by its very existence, even though that hotel operated at a loss. He caused men and women for generations on to remember his years at Sylvan Beach

as the greatest in that village's history. The Cavana Era
was an ideal as much as it became a reality.

Martin and his wife Sarah had no heirs. Their one
son died young. Sylvan Beach was Cavana's child.

It is only fitting and proper that Martin Cavana's
name grace this chapter's title. He was these years in
Beach history.

Art Mengel, a life long Beach resident, said:

> He was Dr. Cavana and everything came out from
> him.

*   *   *   *   *

The Sylvan Beach Running News, 1893
— Taken from Our Local Tabloids —

April 24, 1893 — Our lake's ice went out today. One
gentleman measured the height of a beach ice pile as
being six feet.

May 3, 1893 — Fishing for pike has proved excellent for
the past four days. Just yesterday Harmie Roberts
landed eighteen of the finny beauties at the river
mouth.

May 20 — Miss Grace Barse, who has been attending
school at Oneida, is at home this week with mumps.
Our Sunday School Society will observe Children's
Day.

Adam Miller, Jr., has his new home well under way.
It is Queen Anne style and will be dandy.

As that welcome warmth of spring envelops us, people
are beginning preparations for the upcoming season.
Mr. Garvin has commenced installation of sparkling
gaslights at the already decorous Algonquin. Many
more village improvements are on the way.[3]

*   *   *   *   *

The "great man," Dr. Martin Cavana, came to Sylvan Beach at a time when the Beach was just beginning

to realize its resort potential. The Spencers were selling acres of land, repairing cottages, serving draft beer, and making a good, solid dollar. The Beach was catching on as an Upstate resort. Dr. Cavana saw this; he could see that things were good and could get much better. He had, in a sense, a vision of things to come, but it was his ambition, that prompted his move to Sylvan Beach.

Throughout the Cavana Era, the "picnic" business provided a foundation for the Sylvan Beach economy. The picnics had their origin in the 1880's. These picnics were not the equivalent to the modern idea of the small, intimate ant-ridden family outing. They were mass gatherings, initiated and promoted by Sylvan Beach businessmen. The Beach's merchants paid a good percentage of the group fare and the group's members (or company, in some cases) contributed the remainder. The results of this early "chamber-of-commerce" effort were phenomenal. Thousands came by rail to the Beach. Railroad transportation held a position now occupied by the automobile and Sylvan Beach merchants used it to the fullest.

Grandest of all Sylvan Beach picnics was the annual hop growers and workers picnic, held each July.[4] Oneida and Madison Counties once produced immense crops of hops for export and local use in the brewing and food industries. The hop industry was so important and dominant in these counties' agrarian life that it inspired a Hamilton College English professor, Dr. Clinton Schollard, to write a novel, *A Knight of the Highway,* about life in the hop country. Thousands of central New Yorkers made their living off the hop farms, plowing the endless fields, setting tall poles for the clinging vines and, in climax, harvesting the oat of their labor.

The year was 1910. Syracuse newspapers estimated that thirty thousand hop people would frequent Sylvan Beach for the annual gathering.[5] The picnic of 1893 drew

twenty thousand growers and workers and the nation-
ally renowned speaker, Senator David B. Hill.[6] Recall
that Sylvan Beach was just beginning to come into "its
own" in the early 1890's. Twenty thousand persons is an
incredible number for a village emerging from the "retreat" image into the resort mold. For this event beach
merchants erected two new carousels and "tin type"
studios (post cards and daguerreotypes). More expansion would soon come.

It is fascinating that as one travels from year to year
in Sylvan Beach history, journeying through micro-
filmed newspapers, that each hop growers picnic looms
grander than the last and certainly the grandest of all.
What adds humor to the saga is the fact that a picnic
which attracted 25,000 will be billed as being larger than
one, say five years passed, which drew 30,000. Here we
can witness the prosperity ideal, the good feeling of Cavana's time at work. Every year a better year. This is a
sound public relations scheme.

New York's Governor Glynn spoke at Sylvan Beach's
1914 hop growers gathering. Glynn's speech contains a
valuable analysis of the Sylvan Beach "crowd." The
governor orated:

> Gentlemen: This gathering is a striking proof
> of the fact that you can't draw hard and fast lines
> between any classes of American citizens.
>
> After I had been invited to speak here I in-
> quired from the man who tendered the invitation
> what sort of audience I would face. 'At the hop
> growers' picnic,' he informed me, 'you will find
> lawyers and doctors, business men and mechan-
> ics, farmers and dairymen — and perhaps a few
> hop growers.' From which I concluded that the
> hop growers were a hospitable lot and that their
> holiday attracted that dependable person, that all

around good fellow, that very human being, the average American.[7]

Although Glynn's point about no "hard and fast" lines between American classes could be easily debated, his quote from "the man" brings light to Sylvan Beach's nature as an "everyman resort." We shall later see how the Beach was primarily a working class place, but there was accommodation during Cavana's time for the monied also. Throughout history there has been tolerance for all classes of people at Sylvan Beach.

The hop growers' picnic was the largest ever experienced by the Beach. Other groups that patronized this resort included the Carpenters' and Joiners' Association of Schenectady, the Wire Workers of Cortland, innumerable Sunday school, church and "club" groups (the Rome Businessmen's Association, for example), and, further exemplifying the tolerance which permeated Sylvan Beach, the "colored people."

The colored man's picnic was not one for the migrant upstate farm worker. These were city blacks, with money saved to spend on this, their day at the resort. An incredibly festive atmosphere reigned supreme on this day of each year. Thousands of area whites would join the black people for their picnic, attracted by the "Bo-Jangles" dancing, the boxing matches, and the welcome, vibrant spirit of the black man's day.

But not all found this welcome. There are those who have told how their parents kept them home on this day, warning them about the "wild" black man. Total tolerance never exists. But then, there are also those who have always found Sylvan Beach to be too permissive a place. It is a spot for fun, and people's tastes in amusement vary as the persons themselves. The Beach has, throughout its history, been a gay, carefree place. A rousing good time finds institution there, and a rousing good time is not for all.

The picnics brought the good time en maşse. Sylvan Beach opened itself to them. What reactions ensued were but natural.

Literally thousands of upstate people attended these Sylvan Beach-Cavana Era picnics. One such person was the late Lloyd Blankman, formerly of Clinton, New York. Lloyd was reared in Constantia, Scriba's Rotterdam; he was veritably a man of Oneida's soul. His understanding of and ability to communicate Oneida's north shore history were unequaled. but more importantly, he felt akin to the Lake Oneida, the way only a fortunate few are able. Its history was his history.

One evening, over a bottle of Genesee, Lloyd told me of picnic days and their effect on Constantia. He relived them for me, the eager listener.

> The people would drive their old democrat wagons down to town to catch that train for these picnics. You'd be overwhelmed by the number of people who'd meet the train in Constantia. Our town was just a little village then, a church and store and tavern and the usual flock of houses. These people would descend on the village in droves, why they'd come right on out of the hills. They'd park the democrats along the street and board that morning train. Evening comes, they'd be back, tanked up to their ears, louder than the train itself. It wasn't just one night when I was awakened from a nice sound sleep.

Again, the festivity theme comes forth. There was nothing quite like the picnics.

Populism was a radical American political phenomenom in the 1890's. The Populist Party was fomenting

debate, argument and often violence as it crusaded its re-
form campaign across America. Populists ran for public
office and, sometimes, away from an enraged public. In
America, Populism meant controversy, a basic part of the
country's political system. Somehow, some people didn't
see it that way.

On August 24, 1893, the Populists had a picnic at
Sylvan Beach.⁸ General James Weaver, Populist presi-
dential candidate, Mrs. Mary Elizabeth Lease of Kan-
sas, and Judge Kerr of Colorado were the scheduled
speakers. Lease and Weaver were two of the most important figures in the American Populist movement.

There were firey speeches at the Populist Party-
Farmers' Alliance Picnic. Perhaps one of them went like
this:

> My dear ladies and gentlemen:
>
> The troubled America that we know today is
> an America in need of change — great change!
> Only through the efforts of the people — you
> people — can any effective change take place.
> Listen, dear farmers, workers and your wives. Our
> country needs a graduated income tax system,
> heavier on the rich than on the poor. The govern-
> ment should take over the railroads, telephones
> and telegraphs and destroy the monopolies that
> exploit us! You workers, you backbone of this
> nation's economy — you deserve an eight hour
> working day. You voters — you people who make
> this government run — you deserve a free ballot,
> a secret ballot and a fair count in all elections.
>
> Work for these reforms, dear people, and vote
> for the Populist, the people's, party.

To which Mrs. Lease might have added, "What you
farmers need to do is raise less corn and more hell!"⁹

Well, the Sylvan Beach area farmers weren't up for

raising too much hell. Inclement weather plagued the picnickers, lowering the expected attendance, and several speakers didn't show. The Oneida Dispatch, a Republican paper at that time, called the picnic a "magnificent failure."[10] The Dispatch's writers commented:

> The Populist Movement is not one that meets with great favor in this section . . . threats of secession and of rebellion have been heard before and those who listened to them, a little over thirty years ago, have little patience with those who profess such doctrine at this date . . .
>
> The people of Central New York, regardless of party, do not sympathize with such doctrine. They recognize that the government is for the best interests of the majority and is not to be controlled by a few theorists, some of whose teachings crowd close upon anarchy.[11]

Such was the response to Populism by upstate's establishment press.

The fact that the Populist Party chose Sylvan Beach for its upstate campaign draws light to the nature of the Beach's clientele. The Party did not opt for Cooperstown or the spas of Saratoga. Mary Lease was not born for the Gideon Putnam stage. Sylvan Beach was a working class — common people's resort. It has remained so throughout history. Look who visited there. Hop growers and pickers. Black people. Factory workers. Kids from Sunday schools of rural churches. This was the place for the rousing good time. This was an inexpensive resort — a poor man's resort as some have called it. That does not mean it knew no prosperity. That is but a casual, yet accurate analysis of the resort's patrons. And that analysis knows but one exception, which we shall examine shortly.

The great picnics continued throughout the Cavana

era. Their magnitude and importance for Sylvan Beach cannot be exaggerated. The Beach literally burst its seams on picnic days. These were the days of the multitudes, the days of the big buck. All was prosperity, real hard money. Today, Sylvan Beach has one square mile; then, it was perhaps half that size. Put thirty thousand people into that area, fill it with hotels, taverns, fun spots aplenty, and you have one hustling, bustling boom town.

*   *   *   *   *

— Again, The News —

June 24, 1893 — Bruce L. Spencer painted the bridge over Wood Creek last week.

A moonlight excursion ran over the Lehigh Valley Railroad on Tuesday night from Camden to the Beach.

*   *   *   *   *

Martin Cavana's original ambition at Sylvan Beach was to establish a private hospital, a sanitarium. In 1890, he and his brother James founded a hospital in the Markham Block of Oneida; he expanded to Sylvan Beach in 1891. The Cavana Sanitarium, located at the intersection of Park and Thirteenth Avenues, was small by today's hospital standards, having a capacity of thirty-six patients. It boasted two departments, the hospital for "care of chronic diseases" and the sanitarium, for those needing a rest.

Within the building there were two twelve bed wards and twelve private rooms. Massage, galvanism, and "all modern methods of treatment" were used at Cavana's.

Land for the sanitarium was first purchased by Cavana and brother James on August 19, 1890, for seven hundred dollars.[12] James later sold out his interests to Martin (December 9, 1892) and the latter ended up paying slightly less for the property (about six hundred and eighty five dollars). In addition to using the sanitarium for medical purposes, Cavana maintained a school for nurses. Five or six nurses were always on duty at the hospital during its peak seasons.

Margaret McAndrew Spellicy, of Oneida, learned her nursing skills with Martin Cavana. She was the eager, respectful student whose family was close with the Cavanas. Mr. McAndrew, friend to Martin, "got anything he wanted' 'at the Beach.

The McAndrews owned three or four cottages at the resort, their home camp being a lovely gingerbread gothic revival next to Saint Mary's Catholic Church. The family eventually purchased Cavana's sanitarium (1940) and operated it as the Oneida Lake House, a tourist home. They were very much ingrained into Sylvan Beach life.

Margaret remembers Martin Cavana as the "wonderful man" who attracted patients from "all over the country." She marvels at the respect people showed for him — she and her class of nurses would gracefully curtsey as he entered the room. Others, too, "would almost curtsey when he came in." Margaret's most amazing memory of the doctor concerns his charitable side, however. It is the impression received by a sixteen-year-old girl, an image that could not help but last.

Margaret and her friends, after bedtime, would listen through the floor of the sanitarium, listen to the Cavanas below. What they heard was more than the smalltalk that imprisons so much conversation. They heard people come into the Cavana's kitchen, people in need of food. There were hard times at Sylvan Beach, even in the good years, and some families fared worse than others. Cavana gave from his stores so that people would not go hungry in his village. The father figure, the benevolent boss man, was Martin Cavana. He wanted his people to eat.

It seems ideal, unreal, but it happened. One could look on the tactic as benevolence or as politics, for it has been used before to influence loyalties. Dan O'Connell, patriarch of Albany's democratic political machine, used to take truckloads of turkeys to Albany's poor on Thanksgiving and Christmas. Certainly few votes were lost in these maneuvers. To understand the difference between this and Cavana we must again look at the man and his "child." There was far more than politics behind Cavana's charity. Sylvan Beach was "his" — he had no children. He fed his "child" by attracting new business, by aiding older businesses and by actually giving handouts to those in the town who were in need. Certainly he bolstered his power and image by these efforts, but the fact of their benevolent nature remains.

An advertisement for the sanitarium appeared in the *New Century Atlas of Oneida County* of 1907. The ad dealt primarily with Martin Cavana, M.D., who

> was born and reared in Marcy, Oneida County, was educated at Whitestown Seminary, the University of Michigan, and Bellevue Medical College, graduating from the latter in 1872.[13]

Martin Cavana was the sanitarium. He used this position to become Sylvan Beach.

Cavana's Sylvan Beach hospital proved to be a useful tool in promoting the Beach beyond the realms of upstate. Patients from New York, from Philadelphia and Boston, came for the cures and the ease of sanitarium life. These patients often chartered private trains to Sylvan Beach. The Chesebrough family, makers of "Vaseline" products, became acquainted with Cavana through the sanitarium. Cavana persuaded Louis B. Chesebrough, family head, to invest in the Beach. In 1899, Chesebrough financed the erection of the Hotel Saint Charles.[14]

In the summer of '99, the Sentinel reported:

> Mr. Chesebrough is a young man of extensive wealth, and for the past season or two has been a summer guest of Doctor Cavana. He is much pleased with the natural attractions of Sylvan Beach and the hotel is a want that has long been needed at that popular summer resort.[15]

Chesebrough was so endeared to Sylvan Beach that he made provision for the St. Charles to be an everlasting monument to his feeling for the village. His will contained the stipulation that the hotel was to be operated, even at a loss, each year after his death.

What distinguished this "Hotel Saint Charles?" It was an exceptional place for Sylvan Beach, different from any business the Beach had ever realized. Old timers never fail to say "high class" when they reminisce about the St. Charles. With a capacity of over one hundred and fifty guests, the St. Charles emerged as Sylvan Beach's largest resort facility. In 1903, the highest weekly rate for middle-working class Beach hotels was ten dollars. Rates at the St. Charles began at fourteen.[16] The hotel catered to Chesebrough's wealthy city friends and many of like class from upstate. Carriages elegantly conveyed the St. Charles' patrons from the Ontario and Western Railroad Station to the hotel. Sarah, the hotel's black cook, was regionally famous for her varied, delicious cuisine.

Louis B. Chesebrough was "gentleman Louis." When the man fished, he always brought a guide or lackey to remove fish from his hook. He loved his Sylvan Beach though, and his St. Charles was sacred. Chesebrough insured himself against the possibility of neighbors by purchasing much of the land surrounding the immediate hotel grounds. On July 22, 1899, he secured sixteen parcels of the Squire's Block (a tract of surveyed land along the lake front area) from Reuben Spencer for three thousand dollars.[17] Newspapers wrote of the St. Charles as being apart from the hustling din of Sylvan Beach proper. That was Louie's intention per se.

The Saint Charles found publicity in many upstate papers. The Rochester Herald, August 12, 1910, referred to the hotel:

> Cottages may be rented on the lake shore or one may find accommodations at one of the good boarding houses or excellent hotels (of Sylvan Beach) of which the St. Charles is the best and most commodious, being thoroughly modern in its appointments.

The Canastota Bee, June 27, 1914:

> The Hotel St. Charles, situated on Oneida Lake at Sylvan Beach, New York, will open for its summer season June 27th. This popular hotel is a mecca for automobilists, being on the route of the Empire Tours.

The motor car was finally coming into use, but only for the "few." Now, listen to the Syracuse Post-Standard, July 18, 1912:

> At Hotel St. Charles a ball is planned for Saturday night, and at all the other hotels there will be dancing parties for three nights this week.

"A ball." The Saint Charles was in a class by itself at Sylvan Beach.

Until September 17, 1914. On that date a fire, of unknown origin, ignited in the attic of the grand Beach hotel.[18] All was destroyed, as the structure's tinder quality showed through. The Chesebroughs never rebuilt St. Charles. Louis died before the fire and his wife, Bertha, did not share his zeal for Sylvan Beach.

Following the tragedy, the Rome Sentinel editorial-

Wood River mouth at Sylvan Beach. The above shows the river mouth before Barge Canal construction while below is the same scene, transformed by the canal.

The elaborate Saint Charles Hotel, built 1899, destroyed 1914. This was the class hotel of Sylvan Beach. Contrast it with the below photos of comparable workingman's Beach facilities. (Courtesy Bernie Wameling)

The Hotel Leland, on the point. Note the "bare" exterior, in contrast to the Saint Charles. The Leland was eventually moved and became the Lake Shore Hotel. (Courtesy Chesebrough)

A Beach workingman's hotel interior. The dining room is plain, simple and functional. (Courtesy Bernie Wameling)

Jerre Durham, on far left, the primary antagonist in Sylvan Beach's 1911 de-incorporation. Durham was, in this photo, attending an air show sponsored by The Saint Charles Hotel. (Courtesy Bernie Wameling)

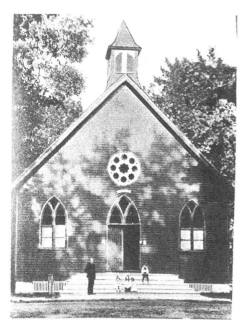

The former St. Mary's Church, Sylvan Beach. (Courtesy Bernie Wameling)

The "unequaled" Nick Honyost. (Courtesy Madison County Historical Society)

The midway, Carnival Park, was a crowded, busy place in Cavana's time. Its entertainment variety was unequaled in Central New York. (Courtesy Bernie Wameling)

This is "Doc" Nichols driving his naptha "yacht." The Niagara, Nichols' boat, was a small version of the huge steamers which toured Oneida. (Courtesy Ed Stewart)

"Black" Bill Dunn's Riverside Hotel. At the same time in Beach history, there was a "Red" Bill Dunn. In spite of first names, the two were brothers. When Wood River flooded, Dunn's Hotel was always found swimming. (Courtesy Glenn Chesebrough)

One of the two "Vienna Villas," alliterated hot dog stands that operated in Sylvan Beach's park. The villas boasted over fifty picnic tables for guests' comfort. (Courtesy Ed Stewart)

Sylvan Beach's Algonquin Hotel — on Wood River, built 1884-1885.
(Courtesy Madison County Historical Society)

Aerial view of Oneida's great east end beach. The beach is much narrower today, due to erosion and the Caughdenoy Dam's construction (which raised lake level one foot). The background of this photo shows the ever-popular toboggan slide and the elongated Rowe Brothers Bath House. (Courtesy Ed Stewart)

The same view, several years later. The boardwalk and Hotel Klippel appear prominent in this roller coaster vista. (Courtesy Bernie Wameling)

One crowded day on the Beach. The toboggan
slide is at left. (Courtesy Glenn Chesebrough)

In a beautifully depth-oriented beach photograph, children pose while adults watch from
water's edge. A tin type studio is in the very rear,
backed by the woods. (Courtesy Glenn Chesebrough)

A family on the cottage porch.

The Cavana Sanitarium, beach front view. (Courtesy Bernie Wameling)

The O & W Station, Railroad Avenue. (Courtesy Ed Stewart)

Railroad Avenue. (Courtesy Glenn Chesebrough)

Frolicking in Lake Oneida

The "Sunshine Makers" Picnic, in the Park.

The old Midway

The Toboggan Slide   (Courtesy Bernie Wameling)

Beauty on-the-Beach

Lakefront pleasures.

Harry Williams was a photographer, a "tin-type man," in Cavana's day. His portraits are colorful, sometimes humorous, likenesses of the people that made the Sylvan Beach of that era a popular pleasure. They come to us today a bit faded, yet still full of their intial life.

(All tin-types courtesy
  Harold Williams)

Posing for Postcards

ized about the St. Charles' value to Sylvan Beach. The paper wrote:

> The loss that comes to Sylvan Beach by the destruction of the St. Charles Hotel is great. It is the greater because the hotel is not likely to be restored, at least with all its excellent features. For the past fifteen years or so this hotel has been maintained, not because of the financial return from its operation, but largely because of a sentiment. It was built by the late L. C. Chesebrough, who died several years ago. He was keenly interested in it and enjoyed it, and his family maintained the hotel since, regardless of the fact that its operation meant an annual deficit. It was a very fine hotel for a place like Sylvan Beach, remarkably well conducted and well equipped. Its management and its surroundings were in contrast with those of other nearby places, and it catered to an element whose wants the rest of the resort did not so well meet.[19]

The St. Charles was a sentiment. Its very existence helped maintain the prosperity ideal that permeated the Cavana era. It made no profit, yet it was the high class of the town, a place that inspired boasting, good feeling and, above all, pride.

Largely through the efforts of Martin Cavana, Sylvan Beach was incorporated as a village "by special acts of the Legislature chapter 812, laws of 1896." The incorporation was reaffirmed by the "laws of 1901, chapter 361."[20] The village's charter, an elaborate document, stated how, through incorporation, the Beach obtained . .

> . . . a police justice, police court, and assessor, a separate highway district of the territory, and health regulations and sanitary improvements,

exemption of the public park from its annual state and county taxation.[21]

Through incorporation, Sylvan Beach had a police justice and a "keystone cops" police force. The village prided itself in the integrity of these men and in the atmosphere of law and order that reigned supreme.

> Perfect order and quiet prevail at this resort at all times during the summer season, where will congregate at certain times upwards of fifty thousand people at one time. We can thank our police force for this, as well as the orderly class of people who frequent Sylvan Beach. Thomas P. Bryant, the Chief of Police, is a state detective and a bonded officer. He has had a great deal of experience and as to his efficiency, we can duly say that during the seasons he has held this position of trust in this place, there have only been three robberies, and every one who was implicated in same were apprehended within twelve hours. Pickpockets are unknown, as when they appear in this vicinity they are invited to accompany the officer to the corporation limits. Bert F. Hosley, Assistant Chief, has held this position for four years, and a very able officer he makes. Nothing can elude him and with his tact and good judgment he can handle as large a crowd as any single individual . . . Courage, tact, and judgment are the three necessary requirements for a guardian of the peace in Sylvan Beach.[22]

The Sylvan Beach Police Department located itself in the village justice building, on a site now occupied by the New York State Police Barracks.

Cavana was one of the village's original trustees (another of that distinguished group was Reuben Spencer.) In 1901, he was unanimously elected President of the

Sylvan Beach Corporation, an office that he would not relinquish until the village incorporation was declared illegitimate in 1911.[23] Through the office of the President, Cavana wielded virtually political "bossman" authority. He had the say in the chartering of new businesses and in the levying of the "corporation tax," a property tax placed on all private holdings. His influence extended into all aspects of Sylvan Beach economic and political life. He was Dr. Cavana and everything came out from him.

Through three real estate investments in June of 1902, Cavana secured ownership of Sylvan Beach's Carnival Park (the amusement area).[24] The Midway of that day sprawled through the area of the point and meandered down along the riverbank. The Algonquin Hotel, which burned in 1899, had its grave decorated in the carnival Midway tradition. Few permanent buildings existed then; the "pitch men" and concession operators arrived each summer, erected their tents and left in early September. "Rollie coasters" and carousels gave thrills and chills to the Midway patrons. The most famous carousel, constructed by Joseph Cottman in 1896, prided itself in its hand-carved German horses and carriages. This carousel was a gilded monument to a gilded era.

To enliven the Midway, Cavana imported high divers of both sexes (the lady being the most popular, of course, since her fall thrust her bathing suit into the liberating breeze). Trapeze artists and acrobats adorned a festive program. Rides in Carnival Park varied from the "Ocean Wave," where people twirled about on a circular, flexible seating platform, to the "Cave of the Winds," a self-explanatory sensation. Artists decorated the rides, one of which was the "Trip to Hell," a voyage into a dazzling mephisto abyss.

Cavana's Carnival Park provides us with an example

of the racism prevalent in America around this time. Old American (not really so old) "nigger booths" found customers aplenty in the Midway. One booth featured a black man sitting on a platform above a water tank. Patrons shot a ball at a target which, if hit, would release the man into the waiting pool. Another booth featured a black man sticking his head out of a large hole in a wall. People paid to throw baseballs at the man. Three shots at the knockout for a dime! Most of the balls the man easily dodged.

Cavana built up and expanded Carnival Park to the point where it became a prime drawing card for Sylvan Beach. Everyone wanted to visit the famed midway at the Beach on the Lake.

* * * * *

July 3, 1893 — The picnic season opened in earnest Wednesday. Over twenty thousand celebrants are expected for gaieties on today's national holiday. One is hard-pressed to find the superlative word for our village's present spirit.

July 10 — There was a balloon ascension at the Beach on Sunday. Instead of one, there were two occupants of the trapeze.

The season at our own Coney Island is now in full blast and picnics and excursions will visit us nearly every day until September 1. Many excursions have already visited us and the Ever Glorious Fourth was celebrated in true patriotic style.

* * * * *

"The unstinted generosity of Nature and Nature's God, seconded by the labor and enterprise of man, has made Sylvan Beach the ideal summer resort of Central New York." As we witness this tune unfold, imagine Sylvan Beach, Cavana's Sylvan Beach, with eleven living hotels, twelve respectable boarding houses, three hundred and sixty home-like cottages, three boat liveries for aqua-cruising as well as angling, electric lights courtesy of Cottman's power plant and, more importantly, people to fill and use these facilities.[25] Imagine these, if you will, as we journey through time back to Sylvan Beach, the Cavana Era.

Come one! Come all! Both large ... and small! I invite you, good people, to venture a journey back to Sylvan Beach, 1907, in the heart of its golden age. Surely you can spare the time for just a short visit to that ever-popular summer resort and its Lake Oneida, most beautiful of New York's inland seas.[26]

Fantastic! You are with us. Now, let's see . . . first let me introduce you to this community's leading citizen, Dr. Martin Cavana. Mr. J. F. Stewart, owner of the glamorous Winsor Hotel — "best location on the lake" — has said that:

> Dr. Cavana is one of the principal property owners of Sylvan Beach and has always associated with public improvement acts, and in the establishing of lawns, cement walks and sea walls, (of which) he was the pioneer Dr. Cavana is the president of the Civil Service Commission of the City of Oneida, Ex-President of the Police and Fire Commission of Oneida, Ex-President of the New York and New England Association of Railway Surgeons, is First Vice-President of the American Association of Railway Surgeons, and for the past twenty years has been the surgeon of the New York, Ontario & Western Railway Company, and it is mostly through his efforts that Sylvan Beach is in a position where its future welfare cannot be gainsaid.

Our village shall be forever grateful to this man for his tireless efforts at community improvement.

If you anticipate staying a spell at Sylvan Beach, you undoubtedly must plan for room and board; our abundant first-rate hotels and smashing restaurants will be more than delighted to serve you. You, the visitor, have the choice of quality.

Consider the hotels. On elegant Park Avenue there are several from which to select. The Darrow House, centrally located facing both lake and grove, has first class board at reasonable rates. George W. Darrow informs us that his establishment is equipped with a boat livery and bathing suits, for the use of all guests. J. Frank Miller's Eagle Hotel, a mere two minutes walk from the O. & W. Railroad Station, has its own steamboat landing on Wood River and a dancing pavilion where everyone makes merry! The Hotel Oneida boasts service unsurpassed anywhere in the region. Now that, my friends, is a boast for the books.

Railroad Avenue is well endowed with places for a night's stay—or more. The Ontario Hotel, opposite the station, is newly equipped and has the most excellent cuisine. Board is by the day or week and, as one guest put it, everything here is exactly as the heart could wish. Griffith Morris, proprietor of the Amsterdam Boarding House, prepares first class meals for his guests for a mere thirty five cents. Beat that, if you can! Mr. Morris has the distinction of being the sole agent for Oneida's popular, delicious Charles House Soft Drinks. At the termination of Railroad Avenue is a hotel we cannot forget. The Forest Home, first hotel of Sylvan Beach, continues in a tradition of success and satisfaction for all who are lucky enough to visit there. This hotel and its reputation speak for themselves.

Sylvan Beach is blessed with a prodigious number of first-rate cafes and taverns where you can whet your whistle and stuff the old innards. As you are walking toward Carnival Park, on Park Avenue, you will notice

right in front of you, at the terminal of said street, the
Silver Dollar Cafe. Call in and see our good friend, Frank
Cole, who is the proprietor, and if he is not there his famous mixologist, Allie Hawley, will do the honors. If
you are in our Municipal Park, enjoying the cool, comforting shade, stop at the two Vienna Villas. These oases
have over fifty open air tables and can furnish you with
the best of tea, coffee, ice cream and lunches. The Lake
View Cafe (guess where this one is!), possessing a truly
appetizing view, will serve you the finest, coldest lager
beer in all of Sylvan Beach. F. R. Chisholm, the proprietor, says that there are plenty of seats and fine breeze
all the time. Take a pleasant walk about our bustling
resort and you will find many other cafes and taverns.
To mention but a few, the Alec Clifford Cafe, Black Bill
Dunn's Star Cafe, Jewell's Restaurant, and the Spencer
Brothers' (yes, they are J. D.'s sons) will all fill the bill.
Now what more can the tired, famished traveler ask?

This year is a momentous one in the history of Sylvan
Beach. The Empire Engineering Company of New York
City is building contract number four of the new Erie-
Barge Canal right in our backyard. This project will undoubtedly bring additional commerce and patrons to our
famous resort. Already, plans are being readied for a
boat, the "Colonial," to sail down the canal from Rome,
bringing eager beach-goers here by the dozen. This canal,
approved by a state-wide referendum in 1903, shall use
the entire length of Lake Oneida for its course. We, at
Sylvan Beach, are proud of this continuing triumph of
man over nature.

We cannot end our tour of Sylvan Beach without a
stop at the famous beach itself. Looking down the beach
from the point, we gaze at the seemingly endless broad
promenade, the boardwalk, stretching from the Leland
Hotel which, by the way, was established in 1896 by
Charles Scoville and operates its own steamer, the "Lot-

tie," to the elegant Saint Charles. Shops along this walk-way, typified by C. M. Williams' Post Cards and Tin Types, provide diversion for the afternoon stroller. The beach itself is famed for its fine, white sand, equalled by no other place in this world. Extending out into the lake is the commodious Rowe Brothers' Bath House, with accommodations and suits for gents and ladies. Prices are always reasonable. The toboggan slides, thrilling spills into ecstasy, are big attractions for bathers and frolickers for miles around. One of the first of these slides at the Beach was erected by George De Long, the well known bathing pavillion man, in 1893. As they said in those days, "it is a corker."

A fitting conclusion to this tour rests in that renown story — "Jolly Old Uncle Josh — His Great Generosity to his Newly Married Niece — A Romance of Sylvan Beach." In this saga, Uncle Josh entertains and guides his niece and "nephew-in-law" through our Sylvan Beach. As Josh was a pretty prolific writer, the story is greatly diluted. We hope you can appreciate the value of Josh's commentary from this sampling. If not, we'll be more than delighted to introduce you to the fellow!

Jolly Old Uncle Josh—A Romance of Sylvan Beach
(Four choice Selections)[27]

"After several fruitless attempts to propose, Charlie broke off in a lamentable stammer. Polly liked him more than he knew and saved the day by softly remarking: 'I've said yes twice, and if you mean it, I do too." This happened way down East, and it wasn't long before there was a wedding. Not much longer before there came a let-ter from Polly's Uncle Josh, out here in New York, con-gratulating Polly on what he termed her spunk and stating that if the young folks would spend the summer with him in his cottage at Sylvan Beach, bordering on

Oneida Lake, he would start them in life, as a wedding
gift, the following fall when they returned to the city. Of
course, they accepted. A few weeks subsequent to the
above happenings, a travel stained party were seen driving on the road towards South Bay, on their way to Sylvan Beach . . .

(The above party arrives, after a fashion, at the
Beach and embarks on a tour with Uncle Josh.
They frequent many places.)

"Oh say, uncle! Where can I go for dry goods?" exclaimed Polly. "This dress does look rather unsuitable,
I must admit." "Well, my girl, if you want to select from
a stock, that for variety and real value is seldom seen
outside of the large metropolitan cities, I will direct you
to Mrs. Sarah Sobey, who keeps a large store in Syracuse.
She has a fine little establishment here at Sylvan Beach,
on the promenade, right next to the Windsor Hotel. She
carries all the latest and fashionable dress goods, and
you are sure to be guided right in your selection. You
will find it pleasant to deal with Mrs. Sobey and the
prices cannot be duplicated." It did not take Polly long
to tell a bargain when she saw one. She got several dress
patterns at very reasonable rates, also all the et ceteras
so dear to the heart of every woman, and Charlie declared she would look particularly swell when the dresses
were made up.

(Josh continues the tour, visiting primarily places
of interest to the male animal. A man of justice,
he rights his wrong.)

"Well!" suddenly ejaculated Uncle Josh. "I think we
have been somewhat selfish over our luxuries, Charlie.
You know Polly never drinks wine or smokes cigars, but
I know from past experience she has an exceedingly sweet
tooth, and here is the place to gratify her desire in this

direction. My friend here (stopping at the elegant display of confectionery offered by D. Musante) is one of the largest manufacturers of confectionery of all kinds in Oneida, and the quality of his goods is equal if not superior to any confectionery sold in Northern New York. His chocolates are the choicest to be had, and the ingredients he uses are absolutely pure and unadulterated. Let us look over D. Musante's elegant display on his stand here in Sylvan Beach, and Polly just order what you want and I will guarantee that hereafter you will call often to see my friend Dave and indulge in his delicious bonbons.

(The group winds up its frolic in fine style)

"Well, it is now about time that we must go over to see my old chum J. S. Cottman, who owns the carousel here in Sylvan Beach, and have a little whirl on his merry-go-round." resumed Uncle Josh. "I tell you children, when I hear the beautiful music emanating from his machine, it brings back old time memories when your Aunt Sally and I used to take all our babys, including you, Polly, down here and even Aunt Sally and I used to enjoy riding with the children. My old friend, Cottman, as one of the pioneers of this Beach, is a most interesting man to talk to and his carousel is the best I have ever seen. We will go there now and watch the dear children frolicking around, and I want to have a little chin with Cottman. When you meet him you will talk with one of the best friends it has ever been my pleasure to make; and we must not forget to see that almost human Jocko, the little monkey, who is one of the most attractive features on the Beach. I must see him tonight as I need rest and he has one of his cottages to rent, right across the bridge, and if satisfactory arrangements can be made, I shall install you children in one of the "best cottages on the Beach.""

Consequently, they were installed.

One wonders how much Uncle Josh lives up to his name. In any case, with a sad farewell, I must end our excursion. Do come and visit us, won't you? The season extends from June through September, so there's plenty of time. We, at Sylvan Beach, are positive you won't regret it.

*   *   *   *   *

July 25 — Charles Bell has added very imposing Greek colonnades to his home, which incidentally houses the village post office. Mr. Bell's addition adds grandeur to the already impressive Railroad Avenue.
The Sunday Schools from New Hartford, Whitestown, Verona, Liverpool, and Solsville Methodist Churches are expected tomorrow for the annual Methodist Sunday School Regional Picnic. Many more people are expected for this gala event.

August 2 — Inclement weather has forced cancellation of outdoor events for the past two days. One man reported, on the lighter side, that those pike were biting like mad in our lake!

August 9 — Rain has dispersed, but cool weather remains. It almost seems that fall advances ahead of schedule this year.

*   *   *   *   *

Lake Oneida has always been a part of, or near, the major trade and transportation routes of New York. Recall that the Erie Canal bypassed the lake, however, and it was not until the first Oneida Lake Canal was constructed that the lake was again connected to an important water route. In colonial days, the lake was an integral part of a major water highway. On November 4, 1903, the people of New York, in affirming the Barge Canal referendum, made Lake Oneida again a part of a great water course.[28]

The Barge Canal (or Erie-Barge Canal, as some call

it) proved to be one grand dualism in the life of Sylvan
Beach. It provided benefit for the village. Immediate gain
was realized from the swarms of tourists who came to
view its construction. The sight of the Empire Engineer
ing Company's immense dredges was unique and people
responded to the uniqueness. The Barge Canal's Sylvan
Beach project produced a half-mile breakwater that became the "pier," a fisherman's dream until its closure in
the 1960's. This brought hundreds of anglers to the Beach
on peak fishing days. The canal also became a water highway for pleasure craft, many of which could travel scores
of its miles, often stopping at Sylvan Beach marinas for
petrol or even a night's stay. In addition, the canal's
cement banks, which ran through the Beach "riverfront,"
acted as a levee, controlling spring flooding of the Wood
River. This latter phenomenon often swamped Sylvan
Beach.

There was a negative side, however, to that canal. Its
dredges, while attracting awed spectators, churned up
mud that Wood River's currents naturally brought to
Oneida. This mud choked the beachfront of its cleanli-
ness, thus repulsing prospective bathers. The mud also
repelled fish, ruining the east shore's normally productive
fishery for several seasons. Fishing and bathing, two
prime drawing cards for the Beach, were temporarily reduced to sidelights. This hurt.[29]

The "great hurt," and this is a subjective matter so
judge it that way, was not immediate. It came in the form
of a life-stripping act. Wood River's mouth at Sylvan
Beach was a place of great beauty. The hickory copses.
The meandering vital river. The arching willows and
elms which formed a green cathedral of the rivermouth.
All these were removed by the Barge Canal's construction. What replaced it has its attractions, financial certainly and probably aesthetic for some, but for this writer
the action takes the form of a deliberate, cruel rape on

the landscape. Sylvan Beach was robbed of a great natural resource. In return it received a linear canal with cement for banks. This was a truly raw deal.

That is my opinion. Sylvan Beachers, at that time, did not view the canal project in such a manner. They honestly thought that the Barge could but help their resort. Ecology, in this case, was subordinated to financial gain.

Throughout the Cavana Era, the New York, Ontario, and Western Railroad was the main railroad line serving Sylvan Beach. The "O. & W." was formed on January 21, 1880, from the organization of the bankrupt Oswego-Midland Railroad.[30] The "OM" had a history of failure, indebtedness, and leaders lacking in foresight. For example, James G. Stevens was hired by the OM in the 1870's to report on the status and potential of its line. His report included the following:

> From Oneida north, the increase in traffic will be slow; the soil is generally poor, the towns small, and nothing that at present can be seen warrants any hope of rapid growth in the future.[31]

The "Oneida north" line ran through Fish Creek Station, one mile from Sylvan Beach.

The O. & W. originally served Sylvan Beach through the Fish Creek Station. Trains transported tourists to this station and steamers carried the vacationers downriver to the Beach, assuming they chose not to walk. Several Beach hotels maintained private steamers to escort guests from the station to piers along Wood River (the Algonquin had a steamer in its day, the Leland sponsored the steamer, "Lottie"). This transferral was awkward and inconvenient, though, and passengers clamored for rail transportation directly into Sylvan Beach. Previous to the Cavana Era, this was achieved. The O. & W. constructed a "loop" from its Fish Creek Station down through the main artery of the Beach. This loop, as you will recall, caused a station to be built, in 1886, on Railroad Avenue. This station was the genesis of the name "Sylvan Beach."

The Lehigh Valley Railroad served Sylvan Beach through a terminal on the Verona Beach side of the Wood River. Originally known as the Elmira, Cortland, and Northern Railroad (E.C. & N.), the Lehigh made connections with the New York Central Railroad, the state's rail aorta, at Canastota. Connections with the West Shore Railroad were achieved at Camden. Throughout history, the Lehigh was but number two at Sylvan Beach. By virtue of location, which brought convenience, the O. & W. carried more passengers, more freight, and therefore earned more profit at the Beach.

Railroad publicity for Sylvan Beach was not restricted to Central New York. Rochester, some hundred miles westward, was very much aware of the Beach and its offings. The Rochester Herald of August 12, 1910, stated:

> Only a short distance from Rochester and easily accessible either by rail or by trolley, lies Oneida Lake, with its broad expanse fringed with pleasant little resorts, among which the most prominent is Sylvan Beach.
>
> ... Sylvan Beach is not a new resort, but it is one of those thoroughly satisfactory places which never lose an iota of their popularity.[32]

The railroads were the means of transportation in Cavana's time, though declining somewhat toward the latter part of the era. Rail publicity, like this, produced.

During the Cavana Era, the "loop" was extended from Railroad Avenue down to the Sylvan Beach river piers. Lake Oneida, in those days, provided a source of ice for the ice-boxes of New York State. Formerly, ice had to be carted, slid, or dragged over a quarter mile of land to awaiting cars on Railroad Avenue. A railroad connection to the river front facilitated ice transportation to the cars, as it is far easier to slide ice over ice than over land.

The installation of this railroad extension was no simple matter. An ecology faction arose in the Beach that voiced the opinion that the aesthetic nature of their river would be destroyed by the railroad. This opinion received strong support in Sylvan Beach, support which prompted a voting down of the railroad line. For the moment, the project oozed in defeat.

Never underestimate the cunning of business, especially when a buck's scent permeates the air. Early one morning, just as the sun was rising, one heard a railman nailing, in Sylvan Beach mellow. All were sleeping, except those railmen nailing. Nailing ties, that later shook, the Sylvan Beachers so.

And they couldn't do a damn thing about it. The railroad extension was there to stay.

In the trek from Utica, Rochester, Syracuse or any major upstate city to Sylvan Beach, Oneida and Oneida Castle Stations constituted the important transfer points. The New York Central and West Shore Railroads intersected the O. & W. at these stations, respectively. Passengers destined for the Beach arrived at Oneida or "Castle" Station and transferred to Ontario and Western northbound trains.

A 1907 time table for O. & W. trains that served Sylvan Beach read as follows:

Main Line — Week Day Trains
Northbound

Leave Oneida	6:10 P.M.	9:20 A.M.
Arrive Sylvan Beach	6:20 P.M.	9:40 A.M.

Southbound

Leave Sylvan Beach	8:23 A.M.	4:45 P.M.
Arrive Oneida	8:43 A.M.	5:10 P.M.[33]

Interim stations (traveling from Oneida) were Durhamville (once an important Erie Canal port), State
Bridge, and Fish Creek. On special picnic days, holidays,
and weekends additional and longer trains were used.
It was not uncommon to hear the rumble of ten-car passenger trains on Railroad Avenue, every car jammed
with "picnickers."

In the pre-auto days, the only other practical means
of getting to Sylvan Beach was by water. Steamboats
puttered between numerous ports on Lake Oneida, carrying local travelers as well as tourists to their aqua-linked
destinations. The largest, most renown of these boats
was the steamer "Sagamore." The boat had a rather
complicated birth. That beginning is simplified below.

The first Syracuse to South Bay (lower South Bay—
near Lake Oneida's west end) Railroad Company began
operation in 1901.[34] The company soon met financial difficulty and William R. Kimball, a primary stockholder
in the railroad, relinquished his interests. Clifford D.
Beebe, an industrialist of Auburn and Syracuse, purchased the company for around a quarter of a million
dollars.[35] Beebe and his associates envisioned resort developments on Frenchman's and Dunham's Islands, and
at the Sagamore Inn of South Bay.

After some alterations and improvements on the
railroad, it was reopened to the public on July 1, 1908.[36]
The line was actually an electric trolley, powered by over-
head cables, and not a railroad per se. The 1909 season
witnessed the Sagamore's christening.[37] This steamboat
made the "run" from South Bay to Sylvan Beach (with
some intermediate stops) in one hour and forty-five
minutes. The Sagamore's capacity was six hundred persons and fare from South Bay to the Beach was a mere
fifty cents. The railroad charge from Syracuse to the bay
was another half dollar.

Around 1925, the railroads began to take a downward

plunge in passenger traffic. Mid-August of that year witnessed a cancellation of trains from Castle Station to Sylvan Beach. August is still a prime tourist month, in any resort's book. Lehigh Valley trains also suffered, but continued serving the Beach for a slightly longer time. There were to be revivals of train excursions in the future as "railroad buffs" in the 30's chartered trains for Beach outings, but the era of great rail business had ended as Cavana's Era drew to a close. "Light business and wishing to use the motor car" eventually stole the grand old passengers trains' lifeblood.

One can follow the gradual decline of railroad touristers to the Beach by reading how the hop people traveled to their annual picnic. In 1900, in the heart of the Cavana Era, 196 O. & W. coaches — 20 different trains — deposited hop picnic celebrants at the Beach.[38] On that same day ten trains, all full, pulled into the Lehigh Valley Station. No other means of transportation deserved mention in newsprint. For the picnic of 1919, the papers reported that, "People came to the beach by train, auto, horse, rig and also via the Barge Canal.[39] The railroad was not exclusive; it had competition in late Cavana years. One competitor, the auto, eventually killed it and, in the process, wrought great change to Sylvan Beach.

Thirty-five licensed passenger steamers sailed the waters of Oneida in July of 1910.[40] The history of steamboats on the Oneida goes back years before Sylvan Beach's founding. Steamboats were built in Brewerton, North Bay and other north shore towns, mainly for commercial purposes. Their prime lake use was in towing barges through the lake as it was impossible for mules to drag the heavy barges along miles of irregular shoreline.

Brewerton probably prospered more from the steamboat building industry than any of the other Lake Oneida towns. J. Elet Milton (re: chapter one, Royal Blockhouse section) and his father occupied prominent positions in that town's ship industry. Milton wrote much of the Oneida steamboats. His writings describe the "Manhattan," a tourist steamer based out of Brewerton. This large craft made the Brewerton to Sylvan Beach trip in roughly two to two and one-half hours. During lake storms, the boat was usually unable to dock at the Beach and would be forced to land in Upper South Bay. From that point, passengers boarded Lehigh Valley (E.C. & N.) trains that ran right to their vacation destination.[41]

In the heat of summer, Milton related, drinking water was at a premium on the Manhattan. The boat carried a huge cask of ice cold water, but this soon abated and passengers clamored for more. It was at that point that the captain pulled a fast one. He ordered the crew to fill the cask with Lake Oneida water, thought to be fever ridden (recall the "lake blossoms" of chapter one) by most passengers. Large quantities of ice were added to the tank and everyone drank freely, "with no thoughts of germs." The affair prompted a musing by Mr. Milton: "Never, perhaps, did water, lake water at that, taste, so satisfying the thirst, better than that drink aboard the Manhattan after an exhausting day at Sylvan Beach.[42]

*   *   *   *   *

August 23 — The coloured people visited our Coney Island today in large numbers. Their gay feeling was much appreciated all over town.

September 3 — The season closed today. There being no services at the church Sunday made the day quite lonely for our people.

*   *   *   *   *

Education, Sylvan Beach Style, The Cavana Era:

W. X. Crider, principal of the Union School, Verona, New York, organized and administered a summer school at Sylvan Beach during the Cavana Era. The summer school served two student types. It provided "teachers

who desire a State Certificate to attend the Summer
School for the entire term of six weeks, and take the State
Examination beginning August 22d, 1898."[43] The con-
glomerate course selection included elocution, higher
math, Greek, Latin, French, German, and music. Tui-
tion costs, six dollars for six weeks, and boarding, available at reduced rates for students, were highly reasonable.

Crider's other school took on a commercial tone. The
"Oneida Lake School" . . .

> Will offer unusual advantages to those who
> wish to prepare office work or as special teachers
> of Penmanship, Drawing and the Commercial
> Branches.
>
> In the Commercial department the students
> will engage in business from start to finish, and
> every entry in their books will represent a trans-
> action that has actually been made.
>
> The Department of Penmanship and Drawing
> is in charge of a man who has had six years ex-
> perience in all lines of drawing for photoengrav-
> ing.[44]

Lessons were available by mail. The school ran from
July 11 to August 19, 1898.

Two active church congregations serviced the people
of Sylvan Beach during Cavana's time. One, Protestant,
the other, Catholic. Union Church, the Park Avenue
congregation, was built in 1887 on land donated by James
Spencer.[45] The church, a summer congregation, was
pastored by many ministers throughout this era, two of
whom were the Reverend Mr. Tillapaugh and the Reverend E. S. J. McAlister. During the "off-season" the
church was the center for numerous "revivals" and sponsored Sunday School programs on Christmas, Easter,

and "Children's Day." Many of the village youth belonged to Union Church's Young People's Society for Christian Endeavor (Y.P.S.C.E.).

Union Church. New England plain outside. Entering the sanctuary and the massive gilded chandelier bursts upon you. Rows of brown benches appear to disagree with it. The grey floor and rustic altar also. Clear glass windows harmonize. Side walls billow out to prepare for the over two hundred crowd. The chandelier is everywhere. All is as it was intended to be. Clean, intact, perfect. An air of preserved grandeur. You know what was here.

In 1899, Father J. B. Mertens established a Roman Catholic parish, Saint Mary's, at the Beach.[46] Mertens was Belgian, educated at the Catholic colleges at Ghent and Mechlin and was graduated from the University of Lourraine. Father Mertens was characterized by his drive and community spirit. Local newspapers labeled him an "energetic and devoted priest." He took an active interest in the welfare of Sylvan Beach and participated in Cavana's chamber of commerce efforts.

St. Mary's was but one of several parishes under Mertens' wing. Saint John's of North Bay and churches at Cleveland and Colosse were also served by the priest. The church building was designed by an architect named Hubbard, of Utica. It was a rustic stave-type of structure, complete with "loft." Heating was unknown at St. Mary's. Old Beach people fondly reminisce of the bone-chilled Sunday masses in late spring and early autumn. They joke of their childhood games in the balcony, only one of its kind in town. Like Union Church, St. Mary's was, at its soul, a community church.

The "antiquated" Saint Mary's Church died in the 60's. Its replacement was a modern brick structure on Route 13, Verona Beach.

In 1896, Sylvan Beach was incorporated as a village. In 1911, through a strange series of incidents, it lost its incorporated status. The scene unfolds this way:

Possibly in 1849, Peter and Phoebe Honyost, Oneida Indians living "somewhere in the Stockbridge Valley" were blessed with the birth of a son, Nick.[47] This Nick Honyost became quite the character, a man whose every word and deed were made of genuine local color. Nick was the alleged champion hop-poler of Stockbridge Valley, setting a boastful 1000 poles in a day's outing. This was no mean feat, as each pole had a six-inch diameter and at least a five-foot height. It may have been legend, but it jived well with Nick's nature. This was a "good nature," influenced much by the joys and stupors of "firewater." Nick was the proverbial town drunk, an "active participant in the judicial merry-go-round." He sang the tunes, played the gilded horses, made merry and probably some Marys, and nearly alway ended up in the clink. The papers called him "Oneida's bilbulous first ward Indian."

Nick flirted with serious trouble in 1905. An Onondaga Indian, for whom Nick had little fond feeling, supposedly threatened Nick and his housekeeper-mistress. A quarrel ensued, turning into a state of duel. The Onondaga brandished a butcher knife. Nick swung an ax. The results you can envision.

Charged with murder, Nick chanced upon the legal services of Durham, Senn and Devitt. The trio emerged victorious in the case, thus liberating Nick to his accustomed life-style. Back to the bottle he went, spreading his good Honyost cheer across the valley.

Now, we advance in the Honyost chronicles to the year 1910. It is July, two weeks before the hop-growers picnic, a true Honyost glory day. On the morning of July 16 Nick boards a train for Sylvan Beach, traveling in his usual intoxicated fashion.[48] Nick was known as a "deadhead" — he road trains on a free Indian pass. Upon reaching Railroad Avenue the train stops, our hero disembarks and lets out a series of air-shattering war whoops! Conveniently, an officer, within steps of the "disturbance," arrests Nick and hustles him off to familiar ground. The next day, Thomas P. Bryant, "keystone" police justice for the Beach, arraigns the hapless Oneida and sentences him to six months in the Oneida County Jail, Rome. With that sentence, the dissolution of Sylvan Beach Village Corporation began.

Here, we must delve into flashback. Jerre T. Durham, the Oneida attorney — the same as defended Nick in his 1905 murder trial — has, to this time, been a close friend to Martin Cavana. Durham assisted the latter in the legalities of constituting the original 1896 village corporation. In return for services and friendship, Durham received all legal work that concerned the St. Charles Hotel. This was no petty fee. He was Cavana's friend and it showed.

The friendship took an abrupt turnabout in 1910. Durham and Cavana had a "falling out" over a business transaction. Durham was embittered by the affair and sought revenge. The Honyost case provided him with the needed opportuniuty. Through his work on the 1896 incorporation Durham realized that Sylvan Beach lacked the required number of residents to become an incorporated village. If Durham could prove that the village was illegally incorporated, Honyost would be a free man, because an illegally incorporated municipality has no right to appoint a police force for self-protection or to sponsor a police-justice, with the power to sentence offenders. Durham had his test case; he set about his task.

And this was not as simple as it seemed. Before Justice P. C. J. DeAngelis of Utica, Durham and Edwin J. Brown, the Beach's attorney, argued the case. Brown contended that "Sylvan Beach was not a village, but a municipal corporation and as such the Justice of the Peace had jurisdiction to hold court there." Durham held staunchly to his position. DeAngelis's decision read:

> It wouldn't be proper for me to strike down the law as unconstitutional at this time of the year and rob the people of Sylvan Beach of police protection. I do not know what I should do after a close analysis of the law, but off hand it strikes me that the Legislature has provided a good, wholesome law for this place and it ought to stand. This legislation is in the right direction and any law-abiding citizen should stand by it.[49]

This was an incredibly incompetent decision. The man admitted ignorance of the law, yet on the basis of mere impression ("it strikes me") he made a decision. Durham was enraged. He brought the case to the Rochester State Court of Appeals.

This re-trial became reversal. On October 17, 1911, the Appeals Court ruled in favor of Nick Honyost.[50] Durham tasted sweet revenge. Sylvan Beach Corporation was no more.

A local paper echoed the decision's meaning.

> The decision is of slight consequence to Honyost . . . but of great importance to the persons who constituted the supposed municipal corporation and who managed its affairs, as it amounts to a decision that all acts that have ever been done in the name of or for the Corporation of Sylvan Beach were illegal and void.

In the beginning of the New York State Legislative session of 1912, Cavana and the Beach's attorneys lobbied successfully for the introduction of three bills that would legalize the affairs of the corporation.[51] The first bill, "for the purpose of legalizing the acts of Thomas P.

Bryant as justice of the Sylvan Beach," the second, for granting "authority to the supervisor and town board of Vienna to collect from delinquent taxpayers unpaid taxes, which were assessed upon property within the boundary of Sylvan Beach by the acting Board of Trustees of the Beach," and the third, which "amends village law in relation to incorporation," all met with failure. Martin Cavana tasted the bitterness of defeat. He and his cronies were faced with ten thousand dollars in bonded indebtedness against the has-been corporation. A part of this was financed through a later tax sale of properties whose owners had been negligent in payment. The remainder became the debt of Cavana and his village trustees.

There exists one point in this story that strikes me as being odd, and that is the relationship between Jerre Durham and Nick Honyost. Durham knew Nick well— he was acquainted with the Indian's escapades, having defended Nick and having resided in the area for years. Nick stopped by Durham's partner's, Judge Senn's, office several times each week to ask for liquor money. Durham certainly saw Nick many times after the 1905 trial. Nick, possibly, was a "plant;" Durham sent him there to be arrested, knowing the destined outcome of the case. It also strikes me odd that Nick would have whooped his piercing cries directly in front of a police officer. The Sylvan Beach keystones were not plain-clothesmen; they dressed in full blue view. But then, perhaps Nick was too drunk or happy to notice. The impressions of "plot" in this case must remain in the realm of speculation.

The 1911 de-incorporation did not alter the economy of Sylvan Beach in any significant manner. Prosperity continued and the Beach functioned in much the same way as before. Many picnics. Thousands of summer visitors. Rides, games, good times galore. The legal hassles

abated with time. The "village" was now the "area" of
Sylvan Beach, a legal distinction only. Cavana retained
the prestige, the holdings, the role as boss man. De-incorporation reduced his official political authority as President of the Corporation (since there was no corporation
now). It was a slap in the face, or sorts, but it did no
lasting damage.

Three barges laden with DuPont gunpowder an-
chored in the Barge Canal on June 25, 1922.[52] Somehow,
they were ignited and the fireworks exceeded any Fourth
of July ever blasted. Thirty-three buildings were destroyed in Sylvan and Verona Beaches. Cottman's electric light and power plant, valued at twenty thousand
dollars, was among the casualties. Total claims against
DuPont totaled over thirty-five thousand dollars. Settlement did not come until years afterward.

Dr. Martin Cavana died in 1924. His estate, valued
at over twenty-five thousand dollars plus property, was
divided among family and favorite causes. Before his
death, he sold his holdings in Carnival Park to Emory
Sauve, Sr. His hospital had lost its leader and, in the
process, its life. No one replaced Martin Cavana as the
benevolent bossman of Sylvan Beach. It is quite prob-
able that no one could. With his death, a gap in leadership was created at the Beach. No longer was there a man
to unite conflicting forces within the village or to promote the Beach with the zeal and success that was Cavana's. Martin Cavana accomplished what no other
person has at Sylvan Beach, making the period from
1891 to 1924 unique in the Beach's history.

These were the "best of times." Sylvan Beach has
known no era like Cavana's. It was this era when the
Beach gained its identity as the workingman's resort.
With this identity came popularity and regional uniqueness, carried aboard scores of railroad passenger cars,

gliding atop steamships on Oneida's calm sea and, most important, implanted in the people's mind. The "Cavana ideal" of prosperity and a "better day around the corner" cannot be downplayed. Its tune cavorted Sylvan Beach through these thirty-some years, making the village dance as it had never before and may never again.

People believed in themselves and in their town. Cavana enabled them to do this. He gave them a "golden age."

Forgive me, Pericles, but the analogy is there.

*   *   *   *   *

— Our Final News —

October 21 — First snow of this year's winter. In honor of the occasion, a new coat was sported by Chauncey Clifford.

November 5 — Eleven and three-quarter inches of frosty fleece fell yesterday, keeping all but the most hardy indoors.

Reuben Spencer made the daring trek to Oneida today. We all wished him luck!

November 19 — We find ourselves imprisoned in the early icy grasp of winter. Even the freight trains run infrequently now. So cold it is. Our beloved summer is but a memory, though a comforting one.

LIVING, DYING, AGAIN AGAIN...

This has been a poor season so far, but we've had poor ones before and we always come up; the visitors and tourists who are our friends always have come back.

—Anna Davis, Auburn Restaurant proprietress, 1951

IV

There were poor seasons and poor years. The years of famine and there were those of plenty. In Cavana's time, the Beach lived and lived well. As time passed, things changed. The Beach lost and then gained and then there was nothing, then something. Things and times changed.

Sylvan Beach lived and died, again and again. It was not a unique experience. The prosperity-depression cycle has touched innumerable American communities. It is an integral part of this nation's being and, therefore, touches even the nation's smallest parts.

The Sylvan Beach of Cavana's golden era died in the second half of the Roaring Twenties. Several factors, local and national, contributed to the decline. One local factor was Cavana's death, which created a gap in community leadership. Seemingly no one could, and definitely no one did replace the good doctor in his unique role of boss man - community promoter. This was the position that made Sylvan Beach; it was now gone. With Cavana's death, all of his financial holdings left the Beach. His sanitarium, a long-time attraction and promotional tool, was forced to close its wards. Cavana's daring and calculating spirit left Sylvan Beach in 1924. This was a grave loss.

1929 witnessed the infamous stock market crash. Reverberations from Wall Street were felt throughout the entire country. Personal incomes dipped, forcing Americans to confine their spending to essentials. Luxuries became even dearer. A resort community's existence is dependent on luxury spending. Vacations and weekend outings are luxuries. Without this form of spending, there can be little profit or reinvestment in a resort community. The community may try to find an alternative income, but this is difficult, as all economy has previously been geared toward one major business — the resort industry. A depression will almost always cripple resort villages.

America's "Great Depression," a time of few luxuries, hurt Sylvan Beach, but could not strangle the village lifeblood from its veins. The depression combined with three other factors, prohibition, rising popularity of the automobile and the basic nature of the Beach as a resort, to produce a "new" Sylvan Beach, a village without a penetrating ideal or stable economy, but with a dogged sense for survival. The village made it through these hard times, scarred, but the better for wear. Let us see why and how this happened.

Sylvan Beach's hotels suffered their death blow even before the depression reached its greatest intensity. The habits of the Beach's clientele were altered by the automobile. In 1920, there were 576,000 registered cars in New York. By 1930, that number had more than quadrupled to 2,330,000.[1] Many more workers and middle class people, mainstay of the Beach's economy, could afford a car in the late 20's. And a car increased their mobility. Now they could travel into the Adirondack Park, the Saint Lawrence Valley, Lake Delta near Rome or virtually anywhere around or out of the state. No longer did they have to board the train to Sylvan Beach for convenient, inexpensive resort pleasure.

The automobile killed passenger trains. A Rome Sentinel editorial of Cavana's time indirectly foresaw the trains' passenger loss. The editorial read:

> The hardest blow to the summer resort business of recent years has been the automobile tour

> habit. The desire to 'see the country' is universal.
> Railroad travel spreads before the traveler a great
> deal of scenic beauty. But it is hot and dusty, and
> in passing through any town, it spreads before
> the traveler a dingy sight of decaying houses and
> coal sheds. Motor travel has enabled people to
> see the beauty of the life of other states and cities,
> and without aching bones and tired heads.[2]

Autos were also a novelty, a new toy if you will for
people's fancy. They caught on fine.

New York passenger trains declined severely in the
20's and early 30's. The long trains of tourists to Sylvan
Beach faded to memory during that era. The O. & W.
cancelled Beach service and closed its Railroad Avenue
station. Every now and then a freight train rumbled
through, cargo laden, but with no hop growers, wire
workers or Sunday School mass gatherings. "Wishing to
use the motor car."[23] The phrase echoed through abandoned O. & W. coaches. Railroad Avenue became Main
Street.

The Lehigh lasted longer in its Beach service, for no
apparent "big profit" motive. Perhaps the railroad just
didn't bother to take time to close its line. In any case,
service was irregular at best, even in summer months.
William Helmer wrote of the Lehigh's swansong at the
Beach.

> The Lehigh Valley connection near Sylvan
> Beach was severed in 1938, leaving the Fish Creek
> interlocking tower just another superfluous build-
> ing. Originally the Canastota Northern, this line
> to Camden had little excuse for existence except
> the vacation trade to Oneida Lake, now gone.[4]

That was the story of railroads at Sylvan Beach. The
tourists came by car.

It was inevitable that the railroads' demise would

bring about a decline in tourism at Sylvan Beach, but it was not so much the decline that ruined Beach hotels. Rather, it was a change in the nature of the Beach's clientele. Gone were the hundreds who came to Sylvan Beach with their trunks, intending to stay for weeks at a hotel or boarding house. Itinerant visitors, people who drove in for perhaps two or three hours, became the rule. A pleasant Sunday drive brought, at times, many to Sylvan Beach. The Beach had always had a large number of "day people," itinerants by nature, but in past years there had been more of them and trains brought them there for the whole day, not just a few hours. Upstate's people found mobility in the motorcar. They used that mobility and the Beach's hotels suffered.

With less business, hotel owners let much of their property deteriorate. Art Mengel, who vividly recalls the "trunk to back seat and a beer" transition at the Beach, characterized the late 20's - early 30's era as a time when people "put a penny in and took a dollar out" of the town. One does not have to be a skilled financier to understand that statement's meaning. Howard Beneke, who moved to the Beach in 1930, talks of the deterioration of the Eagle, a former important hotel. The foundation of that hotel, Beneke recollects, had eroded so much that one could hear the wind whistle through it. Beneke remembered the Midway's "rollie coaster" which, in 1930, shook so much that "you had to get half-looped to enjoy the ride." This was a trait of a town in transition. An old business pattern faded. A new one was emerging. The transition period occurred during a time of national economic recession. There was bound to be an air of decadence in the town. That air, however, was relatively short-lived.

The depression and the auto brought initial ill to Sylvan Beach. This ill was relieved by Prohibition and the Beach's basic resort nature. Prohibition received

AFTER CAVANA

The photos in the next three sections illustrate several aspects of life in Sylvan Beach in the post-Cavana years. Most photos are relatively contemporary, having been taken by myself and my friend Rob Ziegler, a photographer with mighty fine eyes. Rob and I walked through the Beach and its history countless times from the summer of 1972 to the present day. His criticism and encouragement form one of the hidden, unwritten influences in this work. For this, Sylvan Beach and I can thank him.

Pancake House, Main Street

ICE AND THE LAKE

Ice house, West End Brewing Company —
otherwise known as "Utica Club" — around
1910. (Courtesy Ed Stewart)

Ice break-up, spring of 1914, Sylvan Beach. A powerful west wind pushed
tons of ice to the east shore, where it piled enmasse.

Ice Fishermen, December 1972

Russell's Hotel — Danceland was to the rear of this building.

The Sylvan Beach "Skateland," formerly the great
dance hall of Russell's Hotel.

THE SYLVAN BEACH MIDWAY
— NEE "CARNIVAL PARK" —

The Midway in the 1950's

A contrast in the late 1960's

19th century "Beach cagers" pose in a Midway photo studio.

Opening a concession booth

Bernie Wameling, former Midway owner, in the early 1970's

John Clements, concessionaire

Midway patrons

Summer and fall in the 1970's

Rides in the Midway

A Firemen's Convention street musician, 1976.

In an arcade booth

SOME INTERESTING ARCHITECTURE IN AND AROUND SYLVAN BEACH

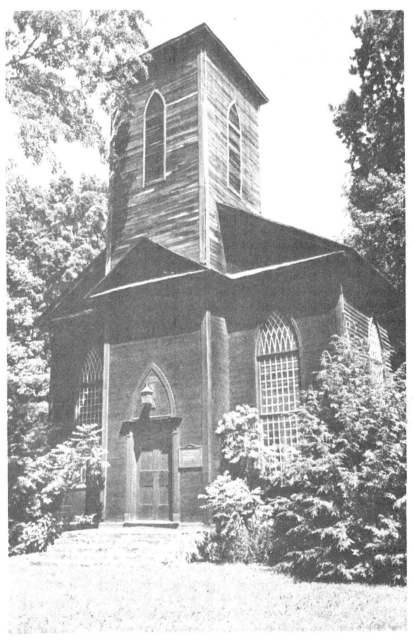

Trinity Episcopal Church, Constantia. Biult on land donated by the Scriba family, this church is one of the finest examples of New York's frontier days structures existing in the region. Its weathered, wooden walls suggest the harshness, yet project the simple dignity, of life in its era.

A gingerbread gothic cottage, along the lakefront in Sylvan Beach. Ornamentation at the peak characterizes this architectural style.

Oneida Lake East Shore Merchants' Association barn sign, Route 13, north of Constantia. This is one of the few barn signs existing in the area. While not an architecture samlpe per se, the barn sign and its structure add a vibrant element to the landscape.

Sunset light brings out the historical flair of the Cavana Sanitarium.

Gingerbread gothic house, Main Street, Sylvan Beach. This is the finest example of this style in the village today. It merits preservation.

legality when, in January of 1920, the 18th Amendment to the Constitution received ratification. This was unique in America, for now the nation was legally "dry." Prohibition, enforced by the amendment's provisions, made the consumption and production of alcoholic drink illegal. The law remained on the books until December of 1933.

Prohibition was a blessing in disguise for Sylvan Beach. Officially, legally that is, it restricted the Beach's numerous tavern keepers. No booze, no bar. But this was not the case. Ingenious barkeepers installed various hiding spots in their establishments, secret compartments for storing beloved moonshine and folksbrew. Customers frequented the bars at known "wet" hours and indulged in heavenly stupor again. Thus, the prohibition institution, the "speakeasy," was born. It was a fraternally clandestine spot for delightful civil disobedience. Sylvan Beach was honeycombed with speakeasies in prohibition years. This was a prime place for Central New Yorkers to water in the "dry time." The Forest Home, among other Beach businesses, was converted into a speakeasy. Its owners knew how to turn a buck.

The Beach was blessed, in prohibition, by loose surveillance by lawmen. There was no Elliot Ness of Vienna township, crime and bottle buster of underworld and under-the-table operations. There were raids, though; one found this description.

Sylvan Beach, August 14, 1933 — The traditional traveling arsenal of the western bad man was outdone by the collection of weapons found when prohibition agents and state troopers raided Samuel LaPorta's spaghetti house last night.

LaPorta, according to the officials, was carrying one revolver in a hip pocket and a second from a shoulder strap, besides a stilleto. In his coat on

the wall was a third revolver, while a rifle and
shotgun were found behind the bar. All the weapons were loaded.

LaPorta and his wife were arrested and taken
to the Utica jail to face Volstead charges. Charges
may also be brought because of the firearms.
LaPorta, according to the officers, is an alien.

Chief Agent Lisle Chesbro said that they
found 12 gallons of whisky, wine and gin.[5]

Sam LaPorta was, proverbially, nailed. Most Sylvan
Beach liquor people were more fortunate. In these times
of great thirst they developed a warning password at
the Beach that would circulate whenever someone heard
a tip for an upcoming booze bust. The Feds or troopers
were coming. Into hiding went the drink. Scurry scurry
went the Beachers, warned by the words, "Murphy's
cows are out!" Here's to it!

Prohibition helped Sylvan Beach, but by far the best
thing this town had going for it in its transition period
was its basic nature as a resort. Sylvan Beach, again, was
and always has been a resort for the working people, the
lower and middle class of society. Other writers call this
group "the masses," a politically undertoned word, but
just as accurate in what it encompasses. The Beach was
a resort for virtually anyone who wanted to visit it. The
"poor man's resort," says Walter Jablonski, a Utica
tavern owner. Look at the prohibition story of Samuel
LaPorta. Here was an immigrant man, an "alien" in the
paper's tongue. At Sylvan Beach he could operate a small
restaurant and function within the village fiber. LaPorta
was but one of the many. The many were the thousands
of Central New York working people who could find in
Sylvan Beach the quality of resort life that was for them,
was them. They could be comfortable here.

By being a "poor man's resort," Sylvan Beach acquired a huge clientele from which to draw its business. This was an asset in the depression years. Even though the auto increased personal mobility and eliminated the convenient trains which brought people to the Beach's heart, it could not obscure the fact that Sylvan Beach was a resort that people could afford. It was no extravagant Saratoga, draped in thoroughbred grandeur. The largest block of consumers in 30's society was attracted to the Beach. This fact, in itself, was enough to keep the resort functioning.

And it functioned, as in Cavana's time, largely through the efforts of concerned public citizens. Sylvan Beach business men took definite steps to improve their lot during the late 20's - early 30's transition years. They founded the Sylvan Beach Board of Trade, a chamber of commerce group, designed to promote the village product. This was the first community effort at "PR" since Cavana's death. It was no Martin Cavana, but it certainly took its philosophy from the good doctor's example. Charles Owler and Isaiah Head served as president and vice-president of the Board.

A glance at the Board's stationery reveals its public relations crusade. That stationery plays up Sylvan Beach as "The Coney Island of Central New York." But a Coney Island needed people, as well as omnipresent hot dogs (a pound of bread, a pound of meat and all the mustard you can eat — for ten cents). Sylvan Beach got those people, on occasion, in the 30's. The steady, regular tourist flow of Cavana's years had departed, but people still came. Sometimes, en masse.

"Yesterday's heat sent thousands of residents into outer sections in search of relief. The sands of Sylvan Beach were packed with bathers . . . " July 23, 1933.[8] Listen to the report from the ever glorious fourth of July, 1935.

> Sylvan Beach, July 5 — State troopers esti-
> mated between 30,000 and 40,000 persons visited
> Sylvan Beach yesterday between 10 A.M. and
> midnight in the greatest turnout in the last ten
> years.
>
> ... The display of fireworks, shot off from the
> lake front near the Lake Shore Hotel, was seen
> by upwards of 5,000 persons, who crowded the
> Barge Canal front, the bridge and the docks on
> the Verona Beach side. The fireworks were spon-
> sored by the Board of Trade.[7]

This was a solid day, certainly successful as far as the
Board was concerned. And there were more of them. In
'35 and '36, the Beach attracted 3,200 and 5,000 persons,
respectively, for the Rome Merchant's Picnic. On July
7, 1934, "thousands swarmed" Sylvan Beach as a mid-
summer heat wave descended on upstate.[9]

Listing these happy days could take pages on end.
They were the high points, the good times again. Fred
Smith, of Utica, remembers them. Fred worked the
amusement stands then. He vividly recalls the steady
streams of autos that blessed the Beach on peak days.
He'd stand by the bridge and count and count and lose
count as the cars poured on. "This was the depression,"
he remembers, "but people came." The black men ,too.
They kept in the tradition of their picnic. They still came
to Sylvan Beach, some 25,000 of them on July 27, 1933.[10]

This was a new Sylvan Beach. It even had a "Miss
Sylvan Beach" in 1933. She was Lila May McCuen. Her
"election" went like this:

> Sylvan Beach, August 18 — Outscoring 40
> competitors for the honor, Miss Lila May Mc-
> Cuen, 30, daughter of Mrs. Blanche McCuen,
> Durhamville, was named "Miss Sylvan Beach of
> 1933," in a beauty contest sponsored by the newly

organized Sylvan Beach Boosters' Club. Miss McCuen was awarded a silver loving cup.

She did not expect to compete in the contest, but rather believed she was to have been one of the judges. It was the first time she had entered such a contest.[11]

A pleasant surprise it must have been. The surprises, as far as the Beach was concerned, were not all pleasant. The village experienced its transition pains in those years. There was a big crowd here, a multitude there, but the economy was irregular, at best.

Business experienced a great ownership turnover in the 30's Sylvan Beach. New business began, with varying success. Howard Beneke started an airport in 1930 — the "Sylvan Beach Airways." Airplanes were a relative novelty then and Beneke hoped to exploit that fact. Pilots, "barnstorming" their way across the country, were treated like kings by awed Americans. Beneke caught on to the "tail" of the barnstorming phenomenon. His airport's uniqueness made it self-sufficient, until Beneke cracked up in 1934 at Panther Lake. The airport, deprived of its airplane, fell into disuse and disrepair. It would never be rebuilt, but oh what a nice idea it was!

William Grant purchased the deteriorated Eagle Hotel around 1934. Grant, a "pitchman" in heart and soul, tried his best at making the old hotel come alive. He brought in gimmicks and loss-leading sales and specials. If there was something to sell, Beach people remember, Grant would sure try to sell it to you. Noisemakers and novelties, kazoos and kitchens, Bill Grant had them all. He was in the hotel business, though, and this had long passed its era. Not even prohibition could help Bill in '34. In 1939, Vincenzo DiCastro bought him out.

Stagnancy and failure far from dominated business at Sylvan Beach during the post-Cavana years. Ronald and Nel McKenzie built their Scot-Noose Park during that era. They chose as their site the grave of the old Saint Charles. On this lot they landscaped, installed dozens of picnic tables and a pavilion, manicured the beachfront and, in general, built a thoroughly respectable park. Scot-Noose developed a reputation for quality service. It attracted, year after year, the Rome business-men's picnic, one of many gatherings at the park. Glenn Chesebrough, a Sylvan Beach "son," portrays Scot-Noose of the 30's as being an ever-crowded, ever-popular place. It certainly was a welcome transfusion for the changing Beach economy.

In 1935, Edward (Eddie) Stewart, of Rome, came to the Beach and purchased Walter Richie's hot dog-ham-burger stand, located on the site of the O. & W. station, Main Street. Gradually, Eddie built a reputation for "just good food," extremely reasonable prices and an original "hot ham" sandwich, a gastronomic delight in anyone's gullet. His business expanded steadily, to its present-day size, the largest restaurant in Sylvan Beach, a restaurant with a regional reputation.

In 1920, William E. Russell, a Yankee immigrant from Stoughton, Massachusetts, established Russell's Hotel at the Beach.[12] "Hotel" is a misleading term, as Russell's was primarily a bar in its years under William's ownership. Bill Russell actively participated in Beach affairs, serving as fire commissioner for some years. He was a popular man in the town and his business pros-pered.

But Russell's grand days were never witnessed by its founder, who died in 1937. In 1939, a dancehall was added to the original hotel.[13] Russell's "Danceland" be-came a household word among Central New York lovers of dancing at its finest. "Taxi dancing," dances where a cuddling couple would pay a dime-a-dance, gained popularity through Russell's Danceland. The fame and fortune of the business, however, soared far beyond the humble taxi dance.

America of the late 20's, the 30's and the 40's, found itself jazzed up and swept off its feet by the era of the "Big Bands." Ah, what a sound it was — mass music, music for all to gear their bodies into a great motion on packed dance hall floors. Benny Goodman, the "King of Swing," Paul Whiteman, the "King of Jazz" and abundant musical royalty toured the country, bandstorming, exciting thousands wherever they played. There was Duke Ellington, "Harlem's Aristocrat of Jazz''and his orchestra, bringing the spirit of the Apollo to American ears. Sinatra had his start in this era. Harry James and Jimmy Dorsey captured the big band sound and implanted their names. These were the "thousand dollar bands," music machines producing the sound that made their people move. They had the country's soul and people felt this soul. The bands notched their place into American history, and as documentors of that history. Technology has let us hear them, though the experience remains in cerebral, at best marginally physical, terms. In each case, the sound is worth the listen.

Russell's Danceland knew the Big Band pace. In the '39 season Whiteman and his "Chesterfield Orchestra" filled Danceland. Just five days earlier Duke and the Aristocrats came, soothing their thousands with "Mood Indigo," "Black and Tan Fantasy" and "Creole Rhapsody." On August 9 of that year, Dorsey jammed the Russell's stage. For this event, cars were lined from Russell's to the junction of Routes 13 and 31, South Bay, four miles from the Beach. The Big Bands made Russell's big.[14]

The late 30's and the 40's were Russell's peak years —music made the scene. There was no limit to musical

variety at Russell's ,as the 30's jazz and swing zeal
evolved into enthusiasm for other tunes. Desi Arnaz and
his "Latin" sound came to Russell's in the 40's. As late
as 1955, Russell's advertised itself as "Central New
York's largest night club."[15] Largest, perhaps, but not
leading. Those days had passed a decade before.

In its heyday, it had no rival. Thousands of upstaters
danced their hearts out at Russell's. Romances sprouted
and blossomed there. Even the place's cuisine was re-
noun. Russell's restaurant prided itself on its "lake pike
dinners." The lake pike, or walleye, is the most sought-
after fish of Oneida. Hundreds of thousands of these
finny beauties inhabit the lake's depths, presenting a
year round angling challenge. Commercially fished during the 30's and 40's, the pike provided local restaurants
with fine table fare. Upstate working people delighted in
the Russell's lake pike dinner. They could afford it and
it was delicious. The hotel's menu further enhanced its
popularity.

Russell's brought dozens of one-day prosperity shots
to Sylvan Beach. On the big-band nights the Beach
glowed as if the Cavana touch had once again descended
on the town. These were but daily affairs, but they were
grand. They pumped vitality into a deserving resort village and they gave thousands of upstate New Yorkers a
night or nights of wonderful fun. What joy there was in
the dancing! I'd have paid a dime for it, and even a quarter for a baked pike on the side.

Upstate New York is no tropical paradise. Its climate
and landscape can be harsh and overpowering. There are
areas of upstate, notably the Tug Hill region and the
Central Adirondacks, where man has lost to the elements
in his battle for prevalence. A drive through backcountry
in these areas, looking at abandoned farms, vacuum-
villages and memory-inhabited logging camps attests

to this lost cause for survival. In spite of his technology and acumen, man could find no place here. Nature was the victor.

The Lake Oneida region has played the role of human garden for years, yet it has been no victory garden per se. Scriba and numerous other early settlers were unable to cope with the region. Their fight for prevalence ended in failure. On into our age nature proved victorious in battle with man.

Oneida has always been a lake to be respected. Colonial travelers, as you will recall, had to bank their hopes on calm days. The west wind brings storms from the Great Lakes, and more importantly, rough, rough water. Listen to this account of a storm on July 16, 1933.

> Sylvan Beach, July 17 — A 47-mile wind, accompanied by a drenching rain, felled trees and wire, put out forest fires and sent lake craft racing to cover about 6 o'clock last night. It was the first downpour of consequence since early May.
>
> Several trees were felled across highways near the resort. Electric light wires were dropped as three maple trees were felled near one place. Cottagers went into the forests which had been burning since Wednesday and found fires were extinguished in some places by the hour and a half rain.
>
> All shipping was tied up as the wind whipped up white caps and spray was driven into the Barge Canal tower on the pier.[16]

The spray reached top windows in the tower, 35 feet above the ground. In 1935, a sailboat operator was swamped on the lake during a similar gale. He was quoted as saying, "We went through four storms at sea while en route from Bermuda to New York, but Oneida Lake had them all beat."[17] Perhaps this is exaggerated, but it does point out the power of a Lake Oneida storm. I have only witnessed them from shore, but even from that vantage point, their magnitude and concentrated natural force produce an overwhelming experience, one that makes a man glad his feet rest on land, enabling him to sit back and see, hear, feel a great force in his history.

There has occurred one fire of note in recorded Beach history. It took a 47-mile-per-hour gale, cited in the preceding lake story, to thoroughly extinguish that blaze. Eventually, the inferno raged over a six-mile expanse, stretching from Poppleton to Jug Point Roads in the Verona Beach area. That region enveloped a bog-scrub forest biome, which had dried out from two months of arid weather. In early June of '33, the bog's nature transformed into tinder. Ignition brought a massive blaze.

The news recorded that blaze, in perfect chronology. It reported:

Sylvan Beach, July 13 — Firemen, campers, troopers and farmers worked side by side last night for hours battling a forest fire burning over a section two miles wide just south of Sylvan Beach and about half a mile off the state highway . . . The blaze illuminated the sky for miles around and hundreds of motorists flocked to the vicinity.

Sylvan Beach, July 14 — After a 40-hour battle with flames which swept bog land between the Poppleton and Jug Point Roads, endangering a school, several camps and a sawmill, the volunteer fire fighters apparently had the blaze under control this morning.

. . . The Talley sawmill, near the school, was in danger from sparks and firemen worked for hours in wetting down the nearby terrain.

When the fire reached within 50 feet of the saw mill, a hurry call was sent out by troopers, directing the fight, to work nearer the building. Trenches were dug. Sand and brooms were used in beating out the flames as they worked nearer the settlement.

All highways entering Sylvan Beach were patrolled by troopers. Motorists were not allowed to park along the highways for fear they would be in the way should the wind suddenly shift.[18]

There was no sudden shift of wind. The fire smouldered on through the sixteenth, when the rains killed it. Man did not beat the fire — it took a rain, a work of the environment, to obtain victory. Man could but "control" the flames, with shovels, guiding troopers, and luck.

Fires burn. Oneida's rough water sprays, capsizes and plays havoc with that which would glide atop its surface. The lake's ice immobilizes. In early December of 1936, a sudden ice storm caused an overnight lake freeze, trapping a fleet of barges.[19] Over three hundred barges were captured by the lake and the Barge Canal system. Icebreakers and thaw rescued most, but several found Oneida to be a cold, damp grave.

Oneida's ice and a tragedy it provoked inspired the nineteenth century upstate poet, Phineas Camp. Camp, a romanticist, composed a volume entitled *Poems of the Mohawk Valley and on Scenes in Palestine,* in which the Oneida frosty verse is found.[20] The title association of the Mohawk Valley and Palestine, sacred Christian land, indicates Camp's bias.

In a preface, Camp explained his poem. A sleigh of young people crossed the lake in mid-winter. Their sleigh fell through a crack or air pocket in the ice, drowning the horses and leaving the people in sorry shape. Two of the group, a young man and lady, were lost from the whole, and made a desperate effort to reach land. When the woman could go no further, her lover abandoned her in hope of finding swift rescue and return. He did return, but too late. His woman was a frozen corpse.

Camp's poem, "Soliloquy of a Female Perishing by Frost":

Haste, Henry, for help, for the chilled and the weary;
I wait thy return in the darkness so dreary;
To the shore of Oneida — Oh, fly! Oh, fly!
Tis hard to forbode, I must die, I must die.

Thou frost wind: Why pour on thy victim thy fury?
From the home of the living, me cruelly hurry?
Thou Ruler of tempests, have pity on me, on me
From thy wrath I appeal unto thee, unto thee.

I fancy I hear the dread wolf at his growling;
Ah, no! Tis the North-wind more pitiless howling—
In the home I have left in my glee, in my glee
Is mother now dreaming of me, of me?

Speed onward, my Henry, to the home of my father,
Where loved ones around the warm hearth-stone
*   now gather*
Then back to my rescue, in haste, in haste;
My life-tide is curdling, quite fast, quite fast.

Oh God of my father, to thee I unburden
They penitent hear; thy suppliant pardon.
O hasten my Henry, return ere I die, I die —
Come—take my last kiss—my sigh, my sigh.

Now, rave ye wild winds, perform your endeavor,
From life and from friends, your victim to sever;
Farewell, O my mother, my father, farewell, farewell,
Tis well with your daughter, Tis well, tis well.

Though Phineas's poetry is not the best, not the best, it provides us with good documentation of Lake Oneida's power. There are no waves in winter, but over the lake travel the same winds, bringing an omnipresent chill and blanketing snow squalls. And the wind is also very sudden.

A man sits in his rented Sylvan Beach 13th Avenue and Main Street room. It is winter now, the time of his first learning. His hyperactive radiator is more than adequate, making the room much too warm. An open window gives outlet and cool to the man as he transcribes his eager tapes. Words come easily and quickly, carrying a freshness and involvement that will last for years. There is calm outside and the clear, crisp air complements his purposeful mental clarity. In seconds, the calm changes to a massive roar, like that of the great falls, only a roar of air, not water. Oneida's west wind brings sudden force to the scene, entering the window as brashly as an always-invited old friend. The man's work continues, its intensity surpassed by the welcome visitor, the inspirer, the natural force which, when appreciated by the man, makes him work so well. This can be a wonderful love affair.

During the thirties and before, a goodly number of Sylvan Beachers profited from the ice business. Refrigeration, in the early part of this century, consisted of icebox freezers and massive ice houses, the latter for large-scale storage. In upstate New York, the neighborhood ice man, complete with horse and wagon, was a colorful street sight. One such ice man even rose to become mayor of Utica in 1960.

Sylvan Beach has always been a good drinking village. It was hardly dry during the thirties and even found itself nicknamed for a glass of beer, the "Sylvan Beach head." Such a glass was primarily head, a foamy white topping for the brewed minority that rested below. You will remember that prohibition brought some discomfort, but certainly little tap corking at the Beach. The beer has always flowed freely here.

Beer, at the Beach, was keg-stored in huge ice-houses, buildings containing hundreds of ice blocks, insulated from summer's sweat by a thick layer of sawdust. Ice for the houses was cut in winter on Oneida Lake and stored for the upcoming season. The lake, which freezes to depths of two to three feet, was a perfect supplier for the several ice firms that harvested its crystal. During Cavana's time, Jonas Cleveland Ice Company and the Rowe Brothers Ice Company monopolized the business. Cleveland was bought out by Charlie Cook, who continued the business through the 30's. After cutting the ice, the Sylvan Beach ice firms would slide their product overland to awaiting railroad cars. From there it was exported to Utica, Rome, Syracuse and sometimes as far away as the lower Hudson Valley when "ice famines," otherwise known as warm winters, occurred there. The Beach's ice factory could never be considered big time, but it created jobs for townsfolk in the off-season, an otherwise drab session for the summer spa.

Let us end the 30's vignette with a myth. In July of 1939 the Rome Sentinel reported:

> Sylvan Beach, July 18—There has been quite a little talk of late in regards to incorporating Sylvan Beach, but the rumor has been denied by I. S. Head, president of the Sylvan Beach Board of Trade, who says he has not heard of any such action being planned and when there is, there will be official notice.[21]

The Sentinel's local columns dealt heavily with gossip and this was just that. It is indicative, though, of the Beach's mood during this post-Cavana time. People were trying to find a panacea for the area's economic ills and a way to adapt to the rapid changes that the resort experienced. It was only normal that some would think "incorporation." The system worked once. It would work again, for a future generation.

The thirties in Sylvan Beach were years of transition. The spirit and money of Cavana's time had departed. Old hotels died, while dance halls sprouted, singing a new song. Passenger trains gave way to the auto, bringing a different kind of tourist to Sylvan Beach. Prohibition brought doses of prosperity, but its repeal in '33 stole the uniqueness from Beach speakeasies. The economy knew no great consistency, yet there were prosperous days and new business was far from unknown. The Beach was still a workingman's resort, but it was not *the* Central New York "poor man's paradise." There were now other places and they were accessible to the masses.

These were different times. This was a different generation. A generation that faced and beat a depression. A generation that had to fight a war.

World War II brought tragedy to the country, to the many families where death showed its ugly head. Sylvan Beach was not exempt from the tragedy. Some of "her boys" made the ultimate patriotic sacrifice. War tragedy took other form, however.

During the war, concentration camps were set up in California and the west to detain Japanese-Americans. People distrusted them. We were at war with their ex-nation and Americans felt that the Japanese loyalty to the United States might waver during the crisis. Japanese-Americans were a small minority and, unlike the millions of German-Americans, could easily be caged and restricted by a paranoia-inspired American people. Prejudice and distrust for the Japanese-American filtered through the entire country.

Verona Beach, across-canal from Sylvan, was the home of Kenneth Iyenaga, his wife and children, and his mother. Kenneth's father, Dr. Toyokichi Iyenaga, was a distinguished scholar and diplomat. Dr. Iyenaga held a Ph.D. degree from Johns Hopkins University and co-authored a book, *Japan and the California Problem*. He was a respected advisor in Japanese-American diplomacy. His name found rest in the prestigious *Who's Who in America*. Dr. Iyenaga died in 1936, a victim of a crack in Oneida's ice.[22] He had been ice fishing.

The Iyenaga family was well-liked and respected in the community. They exhibited an unimpeachable patriotism. In the front window of their Jug Point Road home were a picture of General Douglas MacArthur and an American Red Cross emblem. Kei Iyenaga served on the board of Sylvan Beach's local Red Cross chapter. A portrait of George Washington adorned the Iyenaga parlour wall. There was a Boy Scout Calendar in the kitchen. The family even sacrificed their passenger car for the national scrap metal drive. This was an American family, doing their part for the war effort.

Michael Joseph O'Toole lived at the Beach during this war. "Joe," a retired New York City bartender, tended the liquor counter at Russell's during his retirement years. He was the likeable barman, full of jokes and genial with his patrons. No one could speak a great ill of Joe O'Toole. He was just a nice old fellow.

On the morning of December 23, 1942, genial Joe O'Toole walked into the Iyenaga kitchen, pumped a deadly revolver slug into Kenneth Iyenaga's chest, and critically wounded Kei and her mother-in-law.[23] As simply as he entered the home, Joe O'Toole left, walked to Mrs. Iva Money's grocery, down Jug Point Road, and said:

> I've just shot three people. I want you to call the police.

A shaken, confused character, this Joe O'Toole. He was 64 years old, an old man whose mind had become

twisted and wrought by the war. A state trooper heard
him say:

> The Japs are no damn good.

The Rome Sentinel speculated on his character:

> O'Toole was 'never known as a vicious man.'

That same trooper also testified to these O'Toole
words:

> I'm sorry I didn't get Johnny. I would have if
> he hadn't of run.[24]

Johnny was the Iyenaga's young son.

Michael Joseph O'Toole was tried before the grand
jury. He was found guilty, through an act of "temporary
insanity." Sentenced to an asylum for life, he eventually
died in captivity.

Kei Iyenaga and her mother recovered and returned
to their Verona Beach home. They found much sympathy
there, but the wounds of that cold December morning
in '42 would never heal.

And out west Japanese-Americans continued in their
concentration camp internment. Many, probably most,
of the people were loyal Americans, too.

Sometimes, the sin of the nation affects even its
smallest parts.

The post-war era marked the beginning of prosperous
times for Sylvan Beach. The nation was riding the crest
of a post-war boom. Luxury spending again occupied
most people's summer fancy. It was only logical that the
Beach would profit from this economic resurgence.

In 1947, the functions of the Board of Trade were
taken over by the Sylvan Beach (Oneida Lake) Improvement Association. The Association sponsored such activities as water shows on the canal, mass clean-up cam-

paigns to encourage local pride, and promotion of the resort through advertisement. The 30's Board of Trade used the latter to good advantage for 4th of July galas and related special occasions. The Association's first board of directors were Eddie Moll, Henry Hoffman, Emery Sauve, Jr., Ray Sawner, Sr., and George Esengard. John Aubeuf served as president. Judging from the Beach's economic upturn in the late 40's, the Association's efforts were rewarded.

In the summer of '47 the Association announced plans to expand parking lot facilities at the Beach to a 2,300-car capacity. A 2,000-car lake front lot was proposed, along with a 200-car lot near Russell's and a smaller 100-car enclave near the Barge Canal tower (at the point). The village park received a facelift that summer as fountains and picnic tables found it their new home. These physical upgradings paid off. Note this news account for July 4, 1947.

> Sylvan Beach maintained its high popularity rating as hundreds sought relaxation and made use of the relaxation facilities. Cars jammed the road in the beach area and parking places were at a premium.[25]

Merchants chipped in for a beach cleaning fund in the late 40's, insuring that algae from the lake's eutrophic "bloom" season would be stripped from the sand. Russell's kept up its big-band, big-time image, bringing Harry James in '47 and, as previously cited, Desi Arnaz in '49.[26] This was no small attraction. Beach business began advertising en masse in local newspaper "Drive and Dine" pages. There was no advertising to this scale during the 30's or the war years. In '39, one would be hard-pressed to find ten Lake Oneida establishments advertising in the same issue of the Sentinel. In the late forties, nearly twenty-five lake businesses bared their

wares in newsprint. That's a two hundred and fifty percent increase. It shows the revived interest among Beach
people in promoting their village and the confidence they
had in advertisement success. The Beach was "getting
on its feet," again, on solid financial ground. The taste
of green had been long in coming.

Sunday, May 22, 1949, marked an important day in
Oneida's recent east shore history.[27] On that day the
Verona Beach State Park opened for a "preview," offer-
ing a state-funded, manicured beach, plenty of picnic
space and, as of the 28th of that year, parking for the
multitudes. The park was a highly attractive place and
offered competition for Sylvan Beach. Being two miles
closer to Route 31, the Park upstaged the Beach for
first crack at customers. Time and time again it was
packed with thousands, while the bathing at Sylvan declined. State funds made Verona Beach Park generally
cleaner that Sylvan Beach could ever afford to be. This
and a mere quarter entry fee made the Park a bathing
monopoly on the east shore. Sylvan still had its amusement and established attractions, but Verona Beach
stole the bathing business right from under its wing. It
was a loss for the Beach, but at this time in the village's
history, such a loss could be easily withstood. The economy was too strong to collapse.

There was time for much fishing in the late 40's Sylvan Beach. I have a personal bias for this pasttime and
relish exposing this bias. Thus, you have the following.

Oneida, June 21, 1949: Members of the Fire
Department smacked their lips and declared
'good' the menu prepared by Deputy Chief Seymour Phillips, the main dish of which was a bullhead, 24 inches long and weighing five and one-
quarter pounds.
The bullhead was caught by Patrolman Mat-

thew Flager of the police department at Willow
Grove, Oneida Lake. The fish was the largest of
the variety caught in the area this year.[28]

Which brings us to the last of the 40's, an interview
recorded around June 28, 1949, and published in the
Sentinel on that date.[29] The paper talked with Tony
Zito, musician of the Beach in Cavana's day. Zito was a
relic of the past, a dated reminder of Sylvan Beach's
golden years. His comments were as incisive as they were
nostalgic. Zito was an observer, in song, of the passing
of an age. He could never read a note of music, yet he
memorized over 1,000 melodies of his time. They played
throughout the interview.

I now take the liberty, some may call it license, of
condensing and re-writing the interview. As it exists, it
is too long and prosaic. Tony Zito deserves better. To
the Sentinel goes credit for all facts, but only the quoted
words. Assume that I am writing in 1949, the present
tense for this interview.

Anthony Zito is a man of music. The songs, the
tunes, the many-stringed harp have been his life. His
voice is a booming baritone that needs no amplification.
He comes from a musical family; his father, Emilio,
was well-known in local vaudeville and his three brothers are renowned area violinists.

"Tony" talks of the past. "In the old days you had to
have the pipes," he remembers. Tony had the talent for
"blasting out," yet not offensively. His voice was his
pipes, nothing more. Microphones, amplifiers, and modern electronic gadgetry are not for him.

The musician concept was different in his past.
"Everywhere a muscian went in those days," Tony recalls, "people seemed to say, 'ah, here comes music.' Today they don't pay much attention with the radio and
juke box to distract them." Many Sylvan Beach waiters

were required to "have the pipes" in Tony's wandering minstrel days. "After the Ball," "Sweet Rosie O'Grady" and "Goodbye My Coney Island Baby" enchanted thousands as the Zito orchestra ("every man a soloist") melodied about the Beach. From the ballroom of St. Charles to the barroom of Black Bill Dunn's, the tunes were heard.

Tony remembers a Sylvan Beach with a boardwalk and businesses facing lakeward, with a thriving carnival park and hotels aplenty. "Now everything faces the road or a driveway so people in autos will be attracted . . . Hotels used to be filled. People, usually whole families, came up for a couple of weeks or an entire day by train or boat. Now they come up for a few minutes," he relates.

"The Beach was a great place for honeymooners, too. Last year a big car drove up outside the hotel where I was playing. The chauffeur hopped out and inquired for me. When I got out to the car, the man inside told me I'd entertained him and his wife when they were on their honeymoon years ago."

"His wife had since died, he told me. Well, I spent the whole afternoon singing old songs for that fellow. His favorite was 'Silver Threads Among the Gold'."

Of late years Tony neither smokes nor drinks. He rises each morning at 6:30 or 7 o'clock and walks around the Beach, reconstructing old scenes. Occasionally, he startles other early morning pedestrians or employees around the hotel by bursting into song. He explains this activity quite simply.

"When it's in you, it's got to come out."

And there went music, one tune, one generation. Sylvan Beach lives and dies, again again.

Now, the fifties. People remember and reminisce about them. It's a natural trait for man to fondly recall the good times, perhaps forget some of the bad, but at least dwell in nostalgia for some part of his life. Sylvan

Beachers, unique among upstate villagers, have nearly all their history within easy oral access. Living in a village that's a mere 95 years old, they are not far removed from most of their history. Some remember Reuben Spencer, others Martin Cavana. The old names have circulated with their parents and grandparents.

Beach people easily remember the "fabulous fifties." This was their most recent, and their last, contact with the spirit and physical realities of their "Golden Age." Over eighty per cent of Beachers recall the 50's, and crack a satisfied smile.[30] These were good years. The village had finally adjusted to its new "transient resort" status. Its businesses were geared towards day activities — quick food diners and restaurants, taverns aplenty, an expanded midway and eager merchants set the stage for a return to the bustle and a toast to an assured good tomorrow.

On July 22, 1951, the Syracuse Herald American paper captured the budding good feeling of Sylvan Beach. In a largely promotional article, the paper painted the Beach with the words "Oneida Lake Resort Hopes to Revive Fame of Turn of Century." Sylvan Beachers hoped and finally realized part of their dreams.

Later, the Utica newspapers described the Beach scene in more objective terms. The papers reported, "At present, Sylvan Beach is regaining some of the popularity of the days from 1900 to the early 20's and there has been rapid growth of camps and cottages not only along the Beach front proper, but on its many wooded side streets."[31] Even the Midway was regaining some of its Carnival Park festivity. A photo of the 1953 Midway was captioned by the words, "concessions and ride operators are reporting business 'good' and are looking forward to a banner season."[32] Their banners flew high throughout this decade.

"Developments Noted at Sylvan Beach." The Rome

Sentinel on June 6, 1955, lauded efforts of the Beach's Improvement Association at village rebuilding. Investments had shot up. People were moving to the town. As the paper said, there "are definite indications that the Beach area may be on the move."

Through a pamphlet promotional scheme, the Improvement Association brought their freshly imaged Beach to the outside world. Thousands of the Association's pamphlets, printed in three varieties, were circulated through upstate. They carried with them the image of the Beach as a clean little resort that literally boomed with headline and happy hangover headache in the season. What follows are excerpts from these pamphlets that bring their spirit to you.[33]

"Nestled on the East Shore of beautiful Oneida Lake, lovely Sylvan Beach has been the playground of Central New York since the turn of the century. Young people still flock to the Beach's swimming, dancing and boating attractions and the older folks find Sylvan Beach the perfect spot to relax or 'live it up.'

"Far famed restaurants and hotels and the sparkling Midway atmosphere at the Beach at night has made the area a favorite spot for vacationers, tourists, and weekend visitors. There's something for everyone at Sylvan Beach. Kids love the Carousel, Fun House and host of other children's amusements.

"The fact that Sylvan Beach is visited by over a million fun seeking folks every summer is proof that the uncluttered clean and varied attractions of the area will keep the Beach one of the most popular entertainment and vacation centers in the state for many years to come."

A mellow introduction to our town that is, but it hits home. We have it all at this Beach. Say you want to fish. H .L. Nichols, Mose's, Markell's and Krahl's offer a complete line of bait and tackle. From that point all you need is a boat — Ray Sawner's livery, located right on Wood River backset, will fix you up in that department. This is a place for service — should you lose equipment in boat livery water, Ray's son, George, will even dive to the deeps to find it. He guarantees no fish, however.

And there is night life at Sylvan Beach. A pleasant evening cruise along the lake's north shore reveals the light show mystique of our Midway. Fishermen say they've seen its lights from as distant as Brewerton. Twenty-two thrilling rides spice the Midway with canned thrill, chill and genuine good-will. For the wine, women and song lovers, the Lake Shore Hotel, Hotel Casino, the Parkview Hotel and the Oneida Lake Hotel will all satiate. And even now, as I write this, the famous Jose Barber Band, featuring Janice Conley as vocalist, appears at Hotel DiCastro. At the Beach we can always dance all night.

Headlines decorated Sylvan Beach in the 50's — "Sports - Fun - Rest - Historic Sites - Scenic Splendors" — "Appearing at the Beach This Summer . . . Named Stars of Radio, Television, Stage and Screen!" — A 2,000 Car Parking Area — "The Playground of Central New York" — "Fun for the Whole Family" — and "Four Miles of One of the World's Finest Beaches!" Where have we heard the last one?

"The Sylvan Beach business area is fully paved for your comfort. No dust . . . No dirt . . . "

And crowds galore, in the happy time 50's. In the summer of 1956, 1,675 cars occupied the Beach's lake front parking lot on one record-breaking day.[34] One 1957 Wednesday "kiddie day" at the Midway attracted over three thousand children.[35] These were typical numbers. Figures hit the thousands with regularity in the fifties.

The Improvement Association, in the spring of 1958,

began a series of community projects to upgrade and expand Beach facilities. They did this for good reason.
They anticipated over one million tourists, again, that
summer.[36]

One million. That breaks down to, at the time, roughly one out of every fourteen people in New York. And
these were not all locals. They came from the country's
hinterlands, too. Some from California, others Ohio.
Even a touch of Florida. There was no great out-of-state
migration to Sylvan Beach, mind you, yet the village was
not a purely local resort. "Sometimes you'd wonder how
these people ever knew we were here," mused Victor
Serby, proprietor of the Sylvan Beach Department Store,
"but they came."

The great mass of the "they" in Victor's statement
was local, though, people from the Syracuse-Utica-Rome
triangle. Who were these people; what were their names?
They were the same workers and middle class people that
have always backed Sylvan Beach. George DeFazio, a
General Cable worker from Rome; Steve Wojick, a
Beaunit Fiber Company employee; Helen Martin, a secretary; Tom Fuoco, a butcher; Armand DeRocco, a
sheet metal worker; Joe Bick, an employee of Utica
Club Brewery, and farmers from county townships, mill
hands from textile mills, electrical workers, white collar
people, they all came to Sylvan Beach. The Quinns and
Taylors and Grassis and Petrillos and Zogbys. The
workingman has always been the mainstay of the Beach
economy.

The 50's were prosperous. Upstate, vitalized by new
industry, was prospering. Utica, Syracuse, Rome and
points in-between knew a comfortable era then. Families
found Sylvan Beach to be a choice spot for their good
times. They had the bucks and spent them there. Again,
over eighty per cent of Beach people remember these
years as those of prosperity. The Beach was not unique

in upstate, not the sole place for a workingman's smiling dollar, but the village presented workers with a good, inexpensive amusement package that the whole family could enjoy. This was tough to refuse.

In August of 1959, demolition began on the old bridge over the Barge Canal.[37] The dated, narrow span had caused numerous traffic bottlenecks in past peak seasons. A new bridge arose in 1960, longer, wider and certainly more streamlined than its predecessor. It was, like many Beach improvements, built in anticipation of continuing prosperity, of the throngs returning next year. After 1959, the people and the good times they brought seldom came back.

What happened on April 13, 1960, was almost an omen. On that day, "the ice went out on Oneida Lake and, pushed by strong winds, it rolled like a glacier over Sylvan Beach. Telephone poles snapped like toothpicks."[68] The 60's did similar damage to this decade blooming resort village. Much of the problem took root in misconception, which made it one incredible frustration. That misconception concerned Lake Oneida.

A Hamilton College student once approached a member of the college's physical education department, asking if he could "fish" as a part of his gym program. Fishing, hunting, camping and the like could be substituted for other, more traditional, sports under Hamilton's "5-6" recreation system. The instructor replied, "Sure, where do you fish?" When the Hamilton man answered, "Oneida Lake — I'm going after walleyes," the coach scoffed, "Oneida Lake! Ugh! Pollution!"

It was a myth, but it penetrated every circle. In January of 1960, an article appeared in local papers entitled "Oneida Lake Called Rising Health Menace."[39] The author of the article deemed the lake unfit for swimming at "certain times" and made reference to diseases which could be caught by contact with the raw sewage which supposedly emptied into the lake.

On August 1 of 1966 the Oneida Daily Dispatch wrote that there was "continued growth of weed and shore pollution" at Sylvan Beach. "Children cannot play on the edge of Oneida Lake in the Verona and Sylvan Beach areas."

Let us understand the sixties as being an era which witnessed a major concern on the part of Americans for their environment. There was great consciousness, and rightly so, about the dirt in the air, about the once clean rivers and lakes now spoiled. Environmental law became an issue and dozens of lawyers turned their efforts toward pollutor prosecution. People read, with justified alarm, articles that predicted the years when earth's resources would be exhausted and man could no longer survive in the smudgeland of his creation. There was, in short, some fear that Rachael Carson's "silent spring" would become a reality.

Sylvan Beach received scads of negative publicity about Oneida's "pollution." These were, and still are, the ecology years, years of green-flagged bumper stickers. Many factories, power companies and individuals were forced to clean up or close operations. Sylvan Beach's pollution, however, was grossly misunderstood. This misunderstanding hurt the Beach badly in the 60's.

Recall that Oneida is a strongly eutrophic lake. Eutrophication means "the natural process of aging of a body of water through ecological succession and enrichment."[40] One might compare Oneida to the small farm pond that fills in each year until it becomes part of the fields. Plant life (algae) chokes the pond and eventually fills it. George Meyers and Phillip Greeson, scientists working in cooperation with the United States Department of the Interior and the New York State Conservation Department, published a report in 1969 entitled

The Limnology of Oneida Lake. The report encompassed an analysis of Oneida's eutrophication.

Greeson and Meyers came to the following conclusions. Nutrients and minerals that enter the lake from rivers, creeks, etc., contribute to Oneida's summer algal "blooms." The lake is in a highly fertile area, surrounded by mineral-rich soils. The lake's nutrient-heavy bottom sediments, its shallow depths (maximum—55 feet), its east-west geographic axis and the mixing of water brought on by the ever-powerful west winds, combine with the heat of summer to promote the algal growths. This algae, as green and annoying as it is, is not a pollutor. It is a natural phenomenon.

Throughout history, people have written of the "lake blossom" of Oneida. DeWitt Clinton, Van der Kemp, Milton, and James Fenimore Cooper. The latter wrote:

> (Lake Oneida is) a broad, dark colored body of water, unwholesome to drink and strongly blended with dark particles which boatmen call 'lake blossoms.'[41]

The blooms have been there, are there and will remain. They seldom affected Beach business until the 60's, until ecology became a newsworthy issue and the rain of negative publicity drenched Sylvan Beach. It is sad about this pollution myth. Its effect on the Beach was devastating.

People were afraid. They stayed away.

The ecology issue was not alone in downgrading Sylvan Beach in the 60's. Throughout its history, the Beach has relied on the "working class family trade" for economic survival. This family trade, lamented the Rome Sentinel in an article entitled "Time to Clean Up Sylvan Beach," was practically non-existent. Instead, the Sentinel claimed, the Beach had become a hangout for raucous teenagers. The paper wrote:

> We believe, judging from what we have seen

and what some of the business people — including tavern owners — tell us, that a concerted effort is being made to 'get rid of the undesirable element which at times have taken over the place.'

With us, as with other folks, the Beach as an attraction has 'gone downward' over a long period of years. We don't know just how much money and effort it will take to re-establish the place as a family resort but we do feel a start is being made.

There have been and are permanent residents as well as those who spend the summer months there who 'will have nothing to do' with the 'Beach proper' because of the element which takes over, especially on weekends.

Old-timers can recall when Sylvan Beach was the principal resort area in this section and how it attracted folks from many places. But, with the passing of years a sort of 'don't care' attitude has prevailed with the "buck grabbers" taking out and never giving.

Now, there may be in the offing a new era in an attempt to make the resort the family type of place it used to be where girls and women would again be safe from what is known as the 'rough element.'"[42]

This piece begs analysis. The similarity between the buck grabbers and the people of the early 30's who "put a penny in and took a dollar out" of Sylvan Beach is noteworthy. As far as safety is concerned, for women, there was no wave of crime at the Beach in the 60's. What happened was that people felt uncomfortable with a change in American culture, a change that permeated Sylvan Beach when some businessmen discovered they could profit from it.

That change can most readily be documented in music. The 60's were years of a great generation gap in America. The Vietnam War split thousands with dissent. There was a "new morality," a far cry to rural puritanism. New music, new sounds grew up with the young as rock concerts and festivals brought thousands in tune with the sound. As much as the Big Bands of Russell's moved youth of their era, so did the Jefferson Airplane and Jimi Hendrix in their time. This was a far cry from the relatively staid sounds of the past, sounds that moved parents of the 60's children. The parents' business was alienated by the new rock. With parents came families and with the former's departure, the family trade died.

Gene Aubeuf, former owner of Gene's Bowling Alley, has known the Beach for his lifetime. He experienced the 60's culture shock. He blames the Beach's economic woes on the influx of "offensive" rock music and, of course, its "element." This culture conflict brought on more negative publicity for the Beach. Combined with the pollution malignment, it was a damning influence.

There was a great and noble carousel at Sylvan Beach, dating back to 1896. Fun-seekers knew it as Cottman's Merry-Go-Round, complete with hand carved German horses. Oom-pah-pah music played through carousel speakers. Children and adults loved this great toy. When Bill Cottman died in the 60's, his niece sold the carousel horses — as antiques. A touch of a good era departed.

In April of 1966 John Clements, of Sylvan Beach, and Jerry Furney, of Syracuse, made an attempt at revitalizing the Midway.[43] They invested time in skull session, worked hard at plans. Neither man is involved, to any significant extent, in the Midway today. Failure was not their fault. The Midway was plagued with multitudinous ownership. No common policy could be reached for area development. There was, in other words, no way to collectively get "out of the hole." Owners would not work together.

Sylvan Beach's half-mile breakwater-fishing pier had eroded and weathered to near its waterline by the late 60's. Several people, as a result, were drowned while fishing during a storm. Waves rolled over the break-water, rolling people into the canal. The state closed the "pier," thus depriving Sylvan Beach of the dozens of anglers who fished it daily. A five-hundred-foot section of the pier was reopened in 1975.

Bingo games ended at Sylvan Beach in the 60's. Legalities closed them, sending hundreds of e-a-g-e-r p-l-a-y-e-r-s elsewhere.

But all was not gloom. In the fall of '68, Wendell Burton and Liza Minelli acted part of the "Sterile Cuckoo" at Sylvan Beach. They kissed on the beach, slept in a cozy cabin and held hands in Union Chapel, all for the American movie-going audience. Beach people felt honored that the film was being shot here, but aside from this honor they received little material gain.

On Sunday, August 9, 1970, the Utica Observer-Dispatch ran a front page spread on Sylvan Beach. The Dispatch wrote:

> It (Sylvan Beach) is a museum relic from the 1930's. The Depression seems never to have left this village. A few sightseers stroll quietly through its streets, looking at buildings and amusement halls the same way people in a city park look at trees. They look without seeing, without reacting.
>
> Through the hollow air a loudspeaker blares. It is a slow-speaking, high-pitched monotone extolling "delicious, luscious lollipops made right here at the Karmelkorn stand. Here is where you get the popcorn with the candy on it. Just come in and say 'popcoooorn'."

It says this over and over with precisely the same inflection. It is a recording.

The article was entitled, "Sylvan Beach — A Last Resort."

Winter, 1970. A heavy snow had blanketed Sylvan Beach. The west wind suddenly arose, spreading drifting covers throughout the town. You could barely see. Street lights were polarized to a glow. Dark figures huddled by, clinging as close to the earth as standing permitted. All was cold howl.

Two men stood in front of Eddie's Restaurant, struggling to liberate a car from the Beach winter. They stopped to rest, breathing heavily, listening to the storm that enveloped them. Its cold, sterile cold, seemed to mean something.

The shorter man shivered his first words, "This Beach, this is the way it always is now. Everything's down. The town's nothing anymore."

"Someone has to do something," his friend answered. "There's a lot to develop here. There always has been. I believe in the Beach — it has to get better than this."

"We care about the village and so do others, but what can we do. We aren't millionaires or miracle-workers. What should be done?"

"There's this friend of mine — he's a lawyer. He says we should incorporate into a village. It worked before, in the good years. It can work now. Incorporation will let us run our town — give us a kind of 'home rule.' It's a chance we must take — this village has absolutely nothing to lose."

So, the story goes, the incorporation movement was re-born at Sylvan Beach, after a seventy-five year slumber. Incorporation had worked efficiently in Cavana's day, but this historical precedent was not the primary

Taxi dancing, in the Park

Louie Serby   1907

Sylvan Beach Department Store

Victor Serby   1972

Park Avenue, near Midway

Bicyclists, Along the Barge Canal

Moe LaBella, restaurateur

Memorial Day, 1975

Ed Stewart, restaurant and
liquor store owner.

A Lake Oneida Sunset, from Sylvan Beach

The Lake Oneida Walleye

Clayton Crandall of Brookfield with a limit catch

Bullheaders, Oneida Creek

Breakwater fishing pier, restored in 1976

Barge Canal pier fishing

A square-rigged brigantine enters the lake at Sylvan Beach.

A summer storm

Lakefront moods

At ice-out

Sailing at sunset, along the east shore

. . . and a different type of watering hole.

motivation behind the Beach "movement." A group of
concerned citizens organized themselves into a "Committee for Incorporation." Their arguments took a very
logical form, deriving all tinder from the Beach's then
depressed state.

Recall that Sylvan Beach was but one community
within Vienna, occupying one square mile of the
rambling country township. Beach property owners paid
approximately 35 % of Vienna's total tax revenues. This
was no small sum. The Committee for Incorporation
made their point that if Sylvan Beach had control of
these revenues, the Beach's governing Board of Trustees
could channel all local funds into the village. The Committee argued that Vienna was not giving Sylvan Beach
its rightful 35% of town services. At that time, in addition, the Beach had no representatives on the town board.
This further enhanced the Committee's position that Sylvan Beach's relationship with Vienna township was not
working to the best advantage of the resort community.

The movement for incorporation must be regarded
as an attempt to improve on an existing "bad" situation.
Sylvan Beach had just emerged from the 60's, a decade
of decadence and decline. There was a negative regional
feeling about the Beach, one that kept people away in
the supposed peak tourist seasons. The beach itself was
often uncleaned, as algae from the eutrophic Oneida
would pile along the shores in the summer "bloom" season. More importantly, however, the Beach people themselves were living with their problem, day by day, and
making little or no effort at improvement. The Com-
mitee for Incorporation sought to rid the Beach of this
stagnant air.

On March 5, 1971, the incorporation issue reached
the referendum stage. Two hundred and thirty-eight Sylvan Beachers came to the polls for the decision. One
hundred thirty-three people favored incorporation. The

wheels were set in motion for village government, again. After sixty years.

With incorporation, a definite renewed spirit arose at the Beach. There was community autonomy now. The village had its own government, consisting of a mayor and board of trustees. A village "We Care" booster club kindled, attracting hundreds to its fold. Village park and beach area beautification programs ran rampant. The "volunteer" zeal hit the village, as citizens rhymed with the words of a man who attempted, in bubbling frustration, to describe the new feeling. "My God!" he exclaimed, "You just can't believe how excited people are nowadays! Why, everybody, everybody's doing . . . doing!"

In June of '72, the Rome Sentinel ran a special insert on the Beach. The insert included dozens of ads, articles on incorporation and its political ramifications, photos, interviews, local color, and even a brief history of the town. Pride engendered this insert, pride emanating from a new generation of Sylvan Beachers. This pride manifested itself in the insert's title:

"Sylvan Beach — Threshold of a New Era."

I can say no more.

THE NEW ERA

One generation passeth away
and another cometh, but the
earth abideth forever.

— Ecclesiastes

An historian involved in serious research on any topic must make every attempt to get on the inside of his subject. The Biblical historian delves into ancient manuscripts and scrolls, looking for clues to religious mysteries. The military scholar searches for battle accounts, from a general's strategy to the diary of a private. Similarly, a local historian writing about a village must acquire an in-depth knowledge of its people and their lifestyle. They are his most important source of information. The local historian must explore the inside of his people, yet must remain apart from subjective involvement. He must be able to objectively detach himself from his subject and draw conclusions, devoid of personal bias and friendship. An historian must never lose his identity by being engrossed within his subject. History must be an objective discipline.

It is the winter of 1980. Much has changed at Sylvan Beach since I first came there in January, eight years ago. Incorporation and its effects have transformed a slumbering resort into a revitalized village. Optimism can be found where once pessimism was the order of the day. Still, however, problems exist. Sylvan Beach people's response to these problems will, by in large, determine the degree of success that the village's "New Era" attains.

The term "New Era" implies a great change in Sylvan Beach. That change has been a rapid one. Public works projects, urban renewal, business investment, home construction and renovation, recreational facility improvement and changes in leadership have all been a part of the New Era. This chapter examines these changes and the problems that challenge current village leaders. It is an ongoing chapter that will continue far beyond this book's publication date, as Sylvan Beach people attempt in their New Era to bring back the good feeling and prosperity of Cavana's golden age.

Business investment and expansion have characterized the Beach's New Era. Shortly after incorporation, the Oneida National Bank opened a branch office at the Beach. The bank's handsome brick structure was a welcome addition to Main Street and the proximity of a bank has fostered other business growth.

The restaurant business has boomed in Sylvan Beach's New Era: construction of several large restaurants and expansion of others contributed significantly to that boom. Among the more notable eateries are Greg's Seafood House and Captain John's Restaurant, both highly renowned for their nautical flair. Family restaurants like Schneible's Inn on Oneida Creek and an expanded Ben and Bernie's have given successful infusions to the Beach's economy. Both places are packed solid in summer season. The Beach's financial fibre has been bolstered in the New Era by new, smaller restaurants. Among these are the Canal View Cafe, Ethel's Coffee Shop, Zola's, The Woodside, and Richal's Pizza House. Although small in size, these restaurants have made significant contributions to community prosperity. They attract people — the lifeblood of the Beach.

In 1975, Dominick Bruno opened Bruno's Beach House on Park Avenue. Bruno, former operator of Three Rivers' Inn, inaugurated his night-club restaurant in grand style. The first two seasons at the Beach House witnessed such noted acts as Sadler and Young, Foster Brooks, Tony Bennett, Rodney Dangerfield, and Tiny Tim. "Dom" Bruno's plans of establishing a successful Las Vegas nightclub evaporated after these years, however, as crowds diminished below the break-even point.

Bruno learned that the Utica-Rome-Syracuse triangle, from which most Beach patrons come, would or could not support his grand schemes. Today the Beach House is used for wedding receptions and related parties and, in the summer season, sponsors live "big band" music, attracting modest crowds. The nightclub is an asset to Sylvan Beach, but it could have been much more.

The year 1979 witnessed great change to a venerable Beach relic, the Long Bar. In that year, Gene and Skip Aubeuf purchased the tavern and embarked on an extensive restoration program. The Long Bar, formerly the Hotel Royal, was a Beach landmark in Cavana's years. The Aubeufs' plans include a building restoration to a turn-of-the-century motif and the establishment of a quality restaurant. An upgrading of the restaurant's grounds, which border the Midway, is also planned. High ceilings, ornamental stairways, and a unique balcony which overlooks the main dining area will gain new life under the Aubeufs' plans. Gene Aubeuf, former owner of the village's bowling alley, reaffirms his faith in the community's future through his investment in "Yesterday's Royal." His investment, done tastefully, should thrive. Sylvan Beach will be the ultimate winner.

Additional business expansion has helped Sylvan Beach grow in the New Era. In 1978 Warren and Pete Rauscher expanded their small village hardware store to a spacious quarter-million dollar facility just outside village limits. The Midway has received an influx of investment in the New Era, ranging from a reopened carousel building to snack shacks and different rides. The village, in the years since incorporation, has acquired two new gas stations, a quick-stop style superette, a barber shop, many modern personal homes, and expanded marina facilities along the Barge Canal's backsets. In no Beach economic sector can one find stagnation.

The two greatest changes in Sylvan Beach since incorporation have been the village's "urban renewal" program, funded through a federal Economic Development Agency (EDA) grant and the East Oneida Lake Water Pollution Abatement Project (sewers), centered in Syl van Beach. These programs, initiated by village officials, are destined to have long range positive effects on the community.

In 1977 Sylvan Beach received an EDA grant for over $750,000. With this money, the Beach installed brick sidewalks and ornamental lighting along Main Street, constructed a decorative, wood-beamed bandshell in the park, reclaimed a large portion of lakeshore and built a lakeside park on the site, ripped up Midway streets and introduced a pedestrian mall, erected a commodious bathhouse on the beachfront, and improved parking facilities in the entire waterfront area.

The immediate effect of EDA was to spruce up and give new life to some decadent Beach areas. The lakefront park replaced an area of blighted shoreline where the lake was, in spots, eroding the Beach's antiquated 1950's parking lot. The brick sidewalks and new lighting gave Main Street an historical, gay-90's flair. Businesses like Aubeuf's "Yesterday Royal" can but add to that atmosphere. The Midway pedestrian mall engendered formation of a Mall Merchants' Association, an organization dedicated to preserving and improving the new setting's quality. The bandshell is used for public concerts each Wednesday night in the summer season; hundreds of music lovers crowd the village on these evenings, seeking their favorite tunes. The bathhouse is scheduled for opening upon completion of the sewer project.

Credit for this dramatic facelift goes to several people. The original EDA conception was masterminded by former village trustees John Clements and Terry Skinner. These men researched the grant application process, consulted appropriate persons, and conceptualized their village renewal abstractions. The result was a professional renewal plan, much of which became reality. Credit for administering the grant and for implementing construction of the project goes to former Mayor Joseph DeFazio and his board of trustees. Their energy brought construction through at a vigorous pace and gave the grant its final reality.

For years Sylvan Beach and neighboring shoreline communities have been plagued with antiquated septic sanitation systems. The Beach area's high water table often combined with this aged system to produce offensive conditions. In addition, the septic layout of Sylvan Beach limited business expansion; large motels and related tourist developments hesitated when considering the Beach. In short, the septic system was unsanitary, unsightly and extremely limiting.

Within a year of this book's publication that condition will have been eliminated. In 1971 Sylvan Beach officials initiated a drive to establish a village sewer system. Eventually, after public referendums and numerous debates on this costly issue, the Beach's project was expanded to include the east shore from Edgewater Beach (North Bay) to Kyser Beach (South Bay) and the south shore from Kyser Beach to a point just east of Lakeport. Construction of the project began in 1975. Completion is projected for 1981. The project includes an ultramodern sewage treatment plant that uses chemical decontamination. The plant's architecture, a variation of collegiate modern, has earned it the nickname "Sylvan Beach University."

Abundant benefits have been and will be reaped by the village from the sewers. The obvious initial benefit is the elimination of the septic mess from Beach life. Another is an improved quality for village waters. Oneida is not a polluted lake, but it and any body of water can certainly use the protective insurance a sewer system offers. A third benefit is the new surfacing village streets received from project funds after roads had been torn up for sewer line installation. A fourth plus is the added attractiveness to commercial development the system gives to the Beach.

The sewer project is an expensive venture, costing over $30,000,000, most of which is funded through government aid. Individual unit rates run in excess of two hundred dollars per year. Beach citizens have complained about the sewer tax. It has risen several times throughout the system's construction and it may rise again. Particularly irritating to village people is the fact that, for the last two years, they have been paying the sewer tax and have yet to be connected to the system. Village officials have countered that inflation has escalated sewer costs severely and that the people's additional payment was necessary.

The sewer project must be judged in terms of its long-range effects. These, beyond a shadow of a doubt, will be positive. Today any community the size of Sylvan Beach must have sewers. The words "progress" and "health" go hand in hand with water pollution control. Beach people will discover that, though their costs may seem high now, they will compare quite favorably with the inflated rates of any system constructed in the future. Most importantly, however, because of sewers the Beach will grow.

A great boon to the Beach in the New Era is the hard-working intelligent attitude of its younger generation. These people are the village's future; their achievements will set Sylvan Beach's course. A look at four of them provides insight into their importance to the village.

Every morning in season, Fred and Marge Testa open their Canal View Cafe at 6 A.M., accommodating fuzzy-eyed fishermen and early commuters. The Testas purchased their building in 1978 from Ruth Sauve, widow of former Midway owner Emory Sauve. They remodelled the structure into a sparkling, first-rate cafe, complete with a delightful view of the lake and Barge Canal. In building their restaurant, they took a risk: a sizable investment was required and the Beach already had four established competitors. Fred and Marge perservered and developed a thriving business, an asset to the community.

The Testas have enriched their town in other ways. Every Sunday in the summer they sponsor a flea market on the shaded lawn adjoining their property. This outdoor bazaar attracts several hundred people each weekend. The lunch counter at the Canal View is perhaps the best forum on the entire east shore for discussing Sylvan Beach promotion. Mention what's going on in the Beach and a lively conversation is guaranteed. The Testas, like many of the village's new generation, relish discussion of community improvement ideas. Fred, the sportsman, expounds a cornucopia of opinions on what's best for the lake. Marge, the pragmatic businesswoman, eagerly analyzes village politics, the village economy, the village in general. Positive dialogue, such as that which occurs in the Canal View, is needed for any community to grow and prosper.

Bob and Elaine Johnson form an integral working element in Captain John's Restaurant. Elaine, in charge of waitresses, and Bob, master of the kitchen, are young people with a dream. Simply put, they dream of one day joining America's highest income bracket and believe that Sylvan Beach is the gateway to their aspirations.

Elaine was born into the Beach's business realm. Her father, John DePerno, is the founder of Captain John's. Her uncle, Larry, was one of the best carnival barkers in the 1940's Midway. John and Larry co-owned the Forest Hotel from 1954 to 1979, maintaining it as a leading Central New York rock music haven. Bob Johnson is no commercial novice, either. After college and a hitch in the service, he came to the Beach and took over a gas station. Although business was good, Bob wanted more. After a year in grease he entered the insurance business, working as an agent out of Camden. While involved there, he went to night school and earned his real estate broker's license and his scuba diving certification. Like Marge Testa, he is a continuing analyst of the Beach economy. Bob and I have spent long hours in zealous talk about how the Beach can and will "make it" in the 1980's. Dow Jones and the *Wall Street Journal* could make no better match than Elaine DePerno and Bob Johnson.

How will the Testas and Johnsons help Sylvan Beach? First, they are smart people, with good business sense. Secondly, they believe in their community's destined success. Thirdly, they are young — they have the energy. When I think of these people, I'm reminded of the words from Ecclesiastes:

> One generation passeth away and another cometh, but the earth abideth forever.
> The sun also ariseth and the sun goeth down, and hasteth to the place where he arose.

The Johnsons and the Testas are the new generation. Their sun is just beginning to rise.

While the New Era has been largely a positive time for Sylvan Beach, the village is not without its problems. For the Beach to realize its full potential, these problems must be addressed and solved.

The most serious dilemma facing Sylvan Beach is political factionalism. 1979 was a particularly bad year for this. From March through June local newspapers thrived on disputes between Mayor Charles Johnson and Trustee Eddie Stewart. Articles playing up this Beach political discord appeared nearly every week. Factionalism at the Beach goes far beyond this, however. Longstanding disputes between past village administrations and the current one continue to smoulder. On occasions a minority group that still opposes village incorporation voices its long-buried wrath. Little cooperation exists among the village booster club, the Oneida Lake East Shore Merchants Association (OLESMA) and the village board. With these three groups rests much of the onus for guiding the village to future success.

Dissent within a community is one thing; it can be a healthy, respected part of the American system. When such dissent disintegrates to embittered argument, devoid of real issue and sparked mainly by personality conflict, then that dissent ceases to provide any useful function. In the upcoming years of the New Era, Beach people must strive to settle their petty differences and work to regain the united front they projected in the time of early incorporation. In unity there is success.

Factionalism is not alone among the Beach's problems. The village booster club, long a mainstay of community vitality, has lost much of its zeal. Such fun, people-oriented events as Monte Carlo Night, Turkeys On Tap Evening and the annual summer Fun Festival are no longer held. The "We Care Village News," once a respected booster publication, seldom hits the presses. OLESMA, that organization which should hold merchants together and unite them in unified community promotion, has had difficulty attracting active members. Its president, Richard Moore, is a bright, energetic man who has organized several successful community advertising schemes but, faced with declining member assistance, his energy is fading. Both the booster club and OLESMA need dramatic turn-arounds to meet the challenges of the Beach's New Era.

Despite the tremendous face-lift received from EDA and the sewer project, the Beach's physical facade needs added change. High village and sewer taxes have brought an onslaught of "for sale" signs to village streets. The Beach is still plagued with a plethora of delapidated, turn-of-the-century camps. These camps mar the landscape, detracting from the renovation around them. A developed village master plan, written by qualified planners and carried out by the village board, might provide the surgery necessary to eradicate these eyesores.

A primary cause of all these village problems is the factor of time. In the brief period from incorporation in 1971 until today, Sylvan Beach has been overwhelmed by change. Millions of dollars in business and government investment have been poured into this village of 900 year-round residents. That's a tremendous amount for a small town. The pace of change, its intensity and scope, was bound to create problems.

Despite the changes and problems, Sylvan Beach continues to run much as it always has. There exists a village continuity that flows each day as people give their town a warm vitality. Sylvan Beach is a genuinely nice town, a good place to live and visit. What follows are some of the people and images that make it that way.

*   *   *   *   *

Victor Serby is the man behind the counter at the Sylvan Beach "Department Store." I met him on my first walk through Sylvan Beach, a walk on the day my research for this book began. It was a cold, blustery January Sunday but Victor Serby's store gave light to the otherwise inanimate day. Hm, I thought, perhaps this man could be my beginning, my first interview. Eagerly I entered the store, exchanged upstate greetings and ordered a finger nail clipper, of which I was desperately in need. Mr. Serby shuffled to the store's rear, dug through boxes and more boxes and found one. "At twenty-nine cents it's a bargain," he soft-sold. Since that day, finger nail clippers have been displayed by the cash register of the Sylvan Beach Department Store. One other has been sold.

The next day Victor and I talked of every business that had come and gone at the Beach. Kern's Hotel, the Casino, a once larger Midway, Russell's Danceland, and the infamous Mr. Ajax of Ajax Popcorn Fritters found new life in our conversation. Poor Mr. Ajax, his culinary greatness was doomed to vanish. He worked thirty years with his wife, delighting thousands with tasty sweets. After his death, the business closed. His wife was willing to continue but Ajax alas! She could not remember a single recipe.

And then the "Jack-in-the-Box" story crept into word. It seems that there was this gentleman named Jack in the early twentieth century Sylvan Beach who had the strange habit of keeping a coffin in his house. He was no undertaker, this Jack, but his "box" cast a strangely morbid air about him. One night, in a joyful stupor, he seduced a young woman and lured her to the confines of his home. This was no ordinary romance. Jack snatched the unsuspecting woman in a flash, dropped her in the coffin and nailed it shut. Objective accomplished, he returned to salooning, his great weakness. His loose tongue must have brought boastful confession, and the girl was discovered the next day. Fortunately for Jacks' sake, and for the honor of local color, she survived.

These are Victor Serby's fond memories of the Sylvan Beach he knew as a child. As his good memories flourish, he provides tinder for the blossoming of like thoughts among today's Beach children. Victor is a friend to the Beach kids. They come to him for candy. His store is a real old-time variety store, the kind of place where a "hangout" might have developed. Halloween lovers would love Serby's.

Once when I was there, three Beach urchins walked in. One wore a life-jacket, needed to ride his tricycle around town. Another hid in her coat. The third, Victor said, was a future Beach entrepreneur. She shows super-8 films in her room and charges town kids a nickel entry-fee.

The children found their candy, all seven cents worth. Then, one noticed my camera. They begged for a picture, fascinated by that fancy gadget that hung from the bearded one's neck. Victor Serby laughed and pronounced his vision of the scene: "Those are real Sylvan Beach kids."

They were fun to photograph.

*   *   *   *   *

Moe LaBella is the proprietor of LaBella's Pancake House, a unique Beach building. Four great Grecian Doric columns dominate the Pancake House's front. Greek Revival architecture, a popular nineteenth century style, endowed homes, public buildings and schools. In most cases, the columns were built in a refined proportion to their building. LaBella's columns, however, defy all sense of propriety, thrusting their majesty into Main Street, creating a bloated grandeur — a "Pancake Temple." Apollo would shudder.

Patrons entering the Pancake House in early morning are greeted by Irene, a remarkable person reputed to be the hardest-working, fastest-talking waitress at the Beach. Around ten o'clock, Moe descends from his upstairs apartment, rested from his night's work. In the past few years, LaBella's has captured the sobering-up trade associated with Beach nightlife. "Breakfast at Moe's" has become an established tradition among Beach night owls.

LaBella's is, above all, a social place, a veritable salad bowl of humanity, attracting people from all walks of life. Around the diner's famed back table can be found ex-boxers, boat repairmen, fishermen, state troopers, plumbers, show girls, carnival hands, students, retirees, and even an occasional author or minister. Each day the regulars come here to mull over the state of the Beach. Conversations can get spirited.

"If you ask me Carter's got to go. He's letting the Russians get away with murder!"

"Who asked you? We were talking about fuel oil prices."

"Well this is more important. The world situation's a mess. And what is Carter doing about it? Nothing! Bring on the Republicans."

"I installed a heat-o-lator in my fireplace the other day. Makes a world of difference. Expensive though."

"He was lucky to ge through the Iowa caucus. Now if Kennedy had really tried . . . "

"Hey! I heard they're catching pike over in North Bay. Hitting sidewinders and eyes."

"Irene! Bring us more coffee!"

On and on and on. At LaBella's they don't just sell pancakes, bacon and eggs. They market the parochialized, yet warm, upstate window on the world.

And the coffee "ain't bad" either.

*　　*　　*　　*　　*

Glenn Chesebrough eats at Moe's. Glenn is a retired custodian of the Central Square School District on Oneida's west end. Like many seasonal Beach folk, Glenn spends his winters in Florida and summers at the Beach. He's an enthusiastic fisherman, a fine amateur archaeologist and an ardent card player. With a background like that, Glenn fits in well at LaBella's.

In spite of all jokes and rumors, Glenn is not related to Louis or Bertha Chesebrough.

Talk to people at the Beach about history and they'll tell you of many willing souls who can "tell you all you need to know." Most of the latter informers prove disappointing. Glenn was one who came through, in spades. He knows Beach history like few in the village, yet goes beyond the knowing stage. He lives his history.

Glenn found documentation for the "old scow place," the first name given to the Beach. He introduced me to the accurate wit of Pomroy Jones and to the writings of Van Der Kemp. He drove me to Brewerton and revealed the wealth of the Milton papers. He told me all he knew. From an historian's viewpoint that is all one can ask, but Glenn gave more.

Along with his digging partner, Bill Ennis, Glenn has explored the bygone worlds of the Iroquois. He seeks out area Indian sites and searches through them for relics. He brought me into the Indian world, through stories of their migrations and adventure, through his collection of tomahawks, arrowheads, pipes and Indian life objects, and through himself, through his enthusiasm for research and his desire to share this experience with others.

"History must be shared," he says. "It belongs to everyone."

Glenn Chesebrough shares his history. His images are not stagnant, withdrawn images. They live through the man and touch those fortunate enough to know him. I am thankful to have been one of these.

*   *   *   *   *

A tree grows through the Cavana Sanitarium porch. It's a big tree that extends cool comfort beyond the bounds of the Sanitarium. It's difficult to imagine a building being built around a tree now, especially in this era of crackerbox housing, but in 1891 someone must have liked the idea. Think of it — a tree used not as an ornament, but as an integral part of the home. The tree was a living element of the man's home.

Cavana's building has deteriorated but his tree is still very much alive.

*   *   *   *   *

Four-thirty on a summer's morning. Margaret Devan awakens to the rude clatter of her alarm. Groggily she strolls to the kitchen, coffee in mind. She stops momentarily to gaze out her lakefront window. The cool July evening has mixed with Oneida's waters, producing a light fog. "A pretty sight — so peaceful," Margaret muses. Just then a car horn blares, shattering dawn's tranquility. Margaret Devan dons her housecoat, shivers through a fifty-yard walk, opens the shop and makes the day's first sale. "Fifty night crawlers—$2.00 please," she informs the red-eyed angler. Another day at South Bay Bait and Tackle has begun.

Margaret and Richard "Red" Devan have operated the east shore's biggest and best fishing supply store for over a decade. Red, a retired Oneida city fire chief, combines native wit and extensive fishing know-how with an unsurpassed story-telling gift to make the shop a successful enterprise. On the above morning, Red was still asleep, tired from an all-night worm picking session. Red takes pride in getting his own bait. He'll bend over for hours picking crawlers; he'll wade through muck and mire to catch crawfish; he'll brave inhospitable weather to draw his minnow seines through the lake. Atop this, he hunts, fishes, traps, and works at least eight hours a day in the shop. For a man in his 60's, Red's an achiever.

South Bay Bait and Tackle is *the* angler's headquarters for Oneida's eastern end. Fishermen from Utica, Syracuse, Rome and points between flock to the shop for supplies or just for Red's omnipresent angling advice. Many a giant pike or record smallmouth bass has been caught and recaptured in conversation around the Devans' comforting wood stove. In shop conversation the mighty steelhead trout leaps wildly, the great white-

tail buck speeds across fields, the wary fox eludes yet
another trapper. At this place one gets a good feeling,
a rare sense of appreciation for the outdoors. Here a
sportsman can find peace.

*   *   *   *   *

The Caughdenoy Dam controls the level of Oneida
Lake. Located in Caughdenoy, a former eel-fishing village on the Oneida River west of Brewerton, the dam
can raise or lower the lake several feet. When it was expanded in the late 40's the dam raised lake level about a
foot, effectively obliterating yards of Sylvan Beach sand.
The shallow east shore was tremendously changed, losing over two-thirds of its substance.

The spring of 1979 brought great flooding to Oneida.
High waters, strong winds and massive ice chunks combined to do considerable damage. State officials took pre-
ventive action for the spring of 1980 and, in the fall of
1979, opened Caughdenoy Dam and dropped the lake
over one foot.

This lowering produced a scene from the past, remarkable in its beauty and nostalgia. The Sylvan Beach
of postcards, with its magnificent sands, emerged from
memory. One could but think of the old promotional
line — "Five miles of the best bathing beach in the
world." A lost natural world reappeared. Small, twisting feeder creeks, normally hidden by the lake, cut their
course through the sand. Scoter and eider ducks com-
peted with gulls for minnows in isolated backwater
pools. Sandpipers picked the sand for insects, their
pointed beaks darting constantly. One could view tim-
bers from old piers, their iron fittings rusted from years
of contact with Oneida. A walk down the Beach was a
stroll through Sylvan's history. Occasionally one can
experience this, an encounter with a living part of the
past — living history. How sweet it was.

*   *   *   *   *

Although it's a busy season, summer at the Beach provides a person with a chance for savoring peace and solitude. The New Era has not thoroughly immersed Sylvan Beach in the maddening din of Lake George or Canandaigua. Weekends are hectic, but weekdays are normally quiet times, close perhaps in mood to the "retreat" concept popularized by James D. Spencer in the 1880's.

One August day I walked through the Beach, observing the mellow scene around me. An elderly couple pedalled a tandem bicycle through the park, sharing mutual joy as they traversed the brick-lined trails. Children frolicked in a creative, wood-sculptured play area, added to the park through EDA. The lake was flat that day, a living mirror. In the lakefront park an old man rested on a picnic table, absorbed in thought. Another man occupied the picture, perched on a pail, fishing on the pier. Nothing was biting that day, but it didn't matter. The fisherman was happy to be there, a part of things. The siren-like call of the gulls, the still air, and the encouraging thought that a ravenous pike might venture by, were enough for him.

The quiet Sylvan Beach takes many forms. A yachtsman washes his cruiser. A jogger samples the early morning cool. Two lovers roll about in sand and leaves on a brilliant autumn day. Squirrels chase up and down the village's oaks, searching for acorns. The sun's rays glisten off a towering beach pine, its needles dampened by a summer shower. The list goes on.

Villages have many sides. A local historian must see them all.

*   *   *   *   *

Saturday night at Marion Manor. As nine o'clock nears, the eager crowd swells. Laughter, smoke and the smell of the buffet fill the room. A juke box blares 40's melodies, inspiring some to dance in anticipation of the

evening's entertainment. This is an older crowd, rem-
nants of the big band aficionados that once jammed
Russell's. They await the arrival of John Newton, Sylvan Beach's multi-talented one-man band.

In his Beach tenure, Newton has gained the widest
following of any area entertainer. His first local job was
at Bob Pickard's Kon-Tiki Restaurant, once the east
shore's old time music capital. When the Kon-Tiki
closed, Newton migrated four miles south to Marion
Manor, a restaurant-marina complex on South Bay.
Here, in the spacious, nautical-motifed main room,
Newton makes his music. On weekends and Wednesdays
vintage tunes like "String of Pearls," "Pennies from
Heaven," and "Harbor Lights" fill the air as Newton's
accordion and rhythm maker keep the beat bouncing.

At Marion Manor one can imagine what the Beach
was like in the "big band" days. The innocuously pleasing melodies. The crush of couples on the dance floor.
A veteran vocalist serenades. Polite applause is given to
a fancy-dancing duo. The raucous rumba of a polka
contrasts with the romantic calm of a waltz. History
plays its tune on every Newton evening.

And, dear reader, you may always "cut in."

*   *   *   *   *

Fishing is a social enterprise. Fishermen love to rap
with one another, talking of the departed big ones, of
their special lure and of the many spots they've supposedly discovered. The fisherman often seems to be a
phlegmatic person, sitting on the bank, waiting for a
bite. "What kind of sport is that?" the unbeliever asks.
"You wish you had the patience," the fisherman re-
sponds. And the argument continues on.

At Sylvan Beach, terrestrial fishing is pretty much
confined to the Barge Canal piers. The piers attract their
regular anglers, especially the "short pier" on the Verona
Beach side of the canal. Here, in the morning and even-

ing, one can find a group of the most dedicated anglers on Oneida. Every day they are there — Steve, Chet, "Smitty," "Teach," Margaret and Norm, Emil and "The Redhead," Henry "Panooch" Panucci and Frank from Bridgeport. They are a closely knit group, enjoying each other's fellowship. Every night "the gang" hashes over such topics as the fate of the Yankees, the state of the American auto, memorable fish tales of yesteryear and, when the occasion arises, they cheer the lucky angler who snags an Oneida Lake "golden trout," the local vernacular for carp. Around sunset the ladies comment on the beauty of old sol merging with Oneida's waters. The men scoff at this, advising their spouses to "concentrate more on fishin' and less on lookin'."

Fish they do, but catching fish is another matter. In the spring and fall the gang lands their share of pike, but the long, hot summer brings fishing doldrums to the short pier. Still, each night, they fish. "Why?" I once asked, in a skeptical tone. "Because we have fun together," Steve responded, "this is a good place to be." The gang voiced concurrence.

I thought about that answer. I walked to my truck, got out a fishing rod, and joined them.

*   *   *   *   *

Memorial Day, Sylvan Beach, May 1977. This is a parade. The bands and bugle corps tromp down Main Street, their music proudly playing. The vast crowd that lines the street applauds appreciatively.

Then, the village organizations march down Main. Politicians lead the way, waving at their constituents from a restored Model-T. Boy Scouts and Cub Scouts, the "youthful" seniors' club, the Veterans of Foreign Wars, and several volunteer fire departments follow, strutting proudly down the boulevard. Floats from local clubs and businesses, none of Macy's caliber but creative all the same, bring up the rear. And, of course, the crowd applauds everyone.

At the end, the crowd files into Main Street, milling around in social comfort until the roar of the heavens breaks forth as jets in formation smash the sound barrier over the Beach at two hundred feet, bringing the spectators to turn their heads skyward and ooh and aah and go on with their milling.

They laugh, joke and wave their flags on this Memorial Day. This is a festive, yet in some ways somber, holiday, a day when war dead are honored. On this day organizers worry about parade coordination, dustied medals of honor are cleaned, families congregate for the parade, and an old soldier dons his uniform once again, recalling his service to the country, hoping that such service will never have to be repeated by another generation.

At noon, Beach people gather for a memorial service. They honor their dead and speak highly, proudly, of the America to which they belong.

It seems like the whole town is on Main Street.

* * * * *

Sylvan Beach is, at its heart, a small town. Even in the busiest days of summer one can never be overwhelmed by civilization there. The pace is an easy one in this place, a place where upstate's hills, water, trees and sky merge to provide the backdrop, the dominating element of the village setting. The Beach is small town America, disguised as a resort.

In this town people do things as they do elsewhere.

Henrietta Cleveland parades her manicured dog, in leisure, around the village park. Being the village historian, she keeps a local news scrapbook.

Ray Yahnke spends his meager free time tending to dock repairs at his mother's small marina. A charitable man, Ray donates his construction skills to the local Lutheran church, helping that institution function.

Roy Blowers, Jr., sells bait.

Bob Igoe edits, researches, and publishes books. The former bookstore owner from Utica invested in a one-third interest in North Country Books, a local history publishing company, and moved the company's offices to the Beach. Bob's lakefront sitting room, in his Edgewater Beach home, makes an ideal setting for studying upstate's local history.

"Red" and "Frankie" do odd jobs for Dominick Bruno.

Cornelius Van Der Linde is a real estate man, the village's largest broker. His home, in the Sandy Point Lane development that he created, comes complete with mementoes of his merchant marine days and with a wall filling portrait of his Dutch ancestors. Van, an original village trustee and former mayor, is a speculator in land development.

Paul Pratt, a retired State Trooper, crafts Kentucky rifles. His guns are masterpieces, impossible for the novice eye to distinguish from originals. Craftsmen like Paul are a vanishing breed in America.

At Mr. Lucky's, most clothes go-go . . . .

"Canvas" John Rauscher works with vinyl. His specialty is enclosing boats and his reputation encircles the lake.

Warren Stone, a local grocer, is a radio personality. During summer weekdays, "Stoney" gives the "Sylvan Beach Weather Report" on WIBX. When it's storming in the city, Stoney usually finds some ray of hope at the Beach.

Chester Mazerowski and friends, "No Hope" and "Little Hope," visit the Beach each January. They ice fish, with spirit. There can be no other way.

Anita Jackson is the village clerk. Her husband, Al, is chairman of public works. They do the village's gut-work.

Dick Sullivan was Sylvan Beach's first mayor, Ed McCarthy its second, Van Der Linde its third, and Joe DeFazio its fourth. Charles Johnson is the current one. Ron Johnson, a trailer park owner; Michaela Knapp, a housewife; Bill Smith, an aluminum siding specialist, and Eddie Stewart, Jr., of similar fame as Sr., the hot ham sandwich inventor, are the village trustees. The boss men, of sorts.

Howard Beneke invents. The owner of Beneke Manufacturing Company patented a Christmas Tree Trimmer and is presently marketing that product. Howard had a snowmobile five years before they came out on the market. Invented it himself, of course. This is an ingenious man.

A decade ago, Pat Goodenow, of Utica, was hired by Jim Donlon to man the microphone at Donlon's "Fascination" game. Since then Pat has graduated from college and became a math teacher. Still, he comes back to "Fascination" each summer. As Donlon explains it, Pat got "sand in his shoes."

Joe Terrier runs a service station.

Mike Mitchell is a game warden and a vigilant one at that.

And many people work every day, sleep each night and have a good time on weekends. They are Sylvan Beach people, a friendly folk, typical of upstate New York. They have a rich history; I have tried to capture it. Now the work is done.

Until tomorrow, perhaps, or another day, until someone else comes to the Beach and researches, rewrites, re-sees, hears, feels the rhythm of that village's history. A beautiful rhythm, indeed.

I hope he doesn't keep silent.

MOVING ON, LEARNING MORE

While we read history
we make history.
—George William Curtis

VI

The written history of a community is never complete. After publishing his work, the historian, if he is true to his title, will continue to research and explore any and all material related to that work. Discovery of new material is no indication of deficiency in a historian's work; rather, it is an ongoing, learning experience that helps to make history the exciting, adventuresome discipline it is.

In the four years since my initial history of Sylvan Beach, I have been indeed fortunate in encountering further data on the subject. Some of it I found in old newspapers in historical society files. Other material came from a variety of fine, fascinating letters from people who read my first book. Still other data emanated from conversations with history zealots who attended the many lectures I gave on Sylvan Beach history.

This chapter, "Moving On, Learning More," contains what I consider to be the most interesting Sylvan Beach history vignettes that graced my research of the last four years. They are arranged chronologically, with each vignette corresponding to a specific era in the Beach's history. As was implied in the above introduction, I have truly enjoyed this new exploration into Sylvan Beach history. Let my joy be yours.

* * * * *

A humorous folk-tale graces the first Oneida Lake Canal's saga. Documented by Marshall Hope, contemporary historian of Oneida, the story concerns the origin of the place-name "Jug Point Road," a Verona township highway that parallels the old canal's course.

Near the "side-cut canal's" (first Oneida Lake Canal's) intersection with Wood Creek was located a popular tavern amongst canal men. Parched from long, hot, slow rides, the boatmen eagerly awaited this tavern rest stop. The canal barge owners, however, frowned on drunken boatmen and, as a result, put the tavern off-limits. Never to be outdone, however, the boatmen rigged up long, pointed poles. When their barges approached the tavern the men would alert the innkeeper. The latter brought out jugs of heavenly brew which the boatmen hooked with their poles, thus never leaving the barges. Money was then tossed to the accommodating innkeeper. Thus, the company rules were obeyed and the canallers' thirsts satisfied. The boatmen got their "jugs" on "the point."

＊　　＊　　＊　　＊　　＊

James D. Spencer made one great mistake in his business life. He thought he discovered oil on his Fish Creek property. Imagine it—oil deposits beneath Oneida Lake's east shore. Derricks drilling and pumping barrels of the black gold. Riches aplenty for the taking. James imagined it. And he got burned.

"Clare," the *Rome Sentinel's* roving rural correspondent, captured the scene at Fish Creek, July 1865.

> I perceive that some little excitement has been caused by the report of 'ile' being struck near Mc-Connellsville, Vienna. Now, striking 'ile' is a big thing, but striking tar is a bigger, and consequently of more importance, therefore I claim the honor for Verona. Tar, or some other substance resembling it, has been produced on the farm of Mr. James Spencer, about one-half mile from the outlet of Fish Creek. Hearing of the discovery, and the various stories circulating about it, I determined to visit the vicinity and

ascertain the truth in regard to it. On my way I fell in company with Mr. Post — a neighbor of Mr. Spencer—when, of course, the conversation turned to oil. Mr. Post informed me that he had found indications of oil upon his land, and wished me to look at it. I readily assented. On our way, visions of a flourishing city, with printing offices and railroads floated through my mind. Mr. Post's land lies upon Wood Creek; it is quite low and wet and is excellent for grass. Water was standing in pools and a bluish scum overspread the surface. I looked at it, felt of it. I could see the water and the scum, but no oil. My air castles were falling, my visions were fading away. For comfort, I turned my face toward the west and struck — not 'ile' — but a bee-line for the tar well of J. Spencer, Esq.

I arrived at his house and with him proceeded to the place where the well was located. The place indicated is fifteen or twenty feet square, and in some places the earth is soft and spongy to the tread. In such spots, covered with a crust of earth of about three inches in thickness, lies the 'tar.' It is of a dark color, greasy and somewhat sticky. When dried, it readily burns. Mr. Spencer has sunk a shaft a few feet, which is filled with water, upon the surface of which gas or air is constantly bubbling up. I have no doubt that this substance proceeds from some matter in the bowels of the earth, but whether a mineral deposit or coal bed, I cannot say. My belief is that it comes from a coal bed. Years ago some of the oldest inhabitants greased their wagons with this tar which answered very well for a substitute. Mr. Spencer informs me that he has frequently ploughed it over, but each successive year found it 'the same nasty hole as ever.'

This was no productive well, yet it captivated imagination and inspired frivolous investment.

James D. Spencer and friends organized the "Oneida Valley Oil Company" in 1866. Having the "fullest confidence in the success of the experiment," they raised $25,000 for drilling. Eventually the company's title was changed to the Black Creek Oil Company of Oneida Valley. Black Creek is a local stream whose source runs near the Spencer homestead. The company drilled through May of 1867 without finding oil. Newsprint optimism and much wet sand were the sole products of this Spencer and Co. venture. There was no 'ile' under Oneida's east shore.

It was a splendid failure, yet it had its humor. For generations after, Fish Creek area children voiced a laughtered warning to their comrades who played around Spencer's well site. "Don't go near the oil well," they'd chant, "or you'll fall down through to China!"

*   *   *   *   *

Cosmos' observations of Sylvan Beach's beginnings are complimented by the writings of W. Hector Gale, editor of the *Oneida Free Press* (1880-1896). Gale maintained a summer residence, "The Maples," at Sylvan Beach. He wrote, in his paper, of the growth of the Forest Home, of the "Beacon Beach" name for Sylvan Beach (which, according to Gale, referred to a beacon set out by James D. Spencer as a guide for sand barges navigating the lake) and of the early picnics that frequented the Beach. Gale himself helped to organize one of these picnics, the annual convention of Oneida City's Civil War veterans.

Hector Gale was an incisive observer and, above all, a man of wit. On August 26, 1882, he published an article entitled "A Day of Pleasure." His prose delved into

BUSINESS EXPANSION

Fred and Marge Testa by their "Canal View Cafe"

Restoration work on "Yesterday's Royal"

Schneible's Inn, Oneida Creek

Greg's Seafood House

Koster's Home Center

Captain John's

Village offices

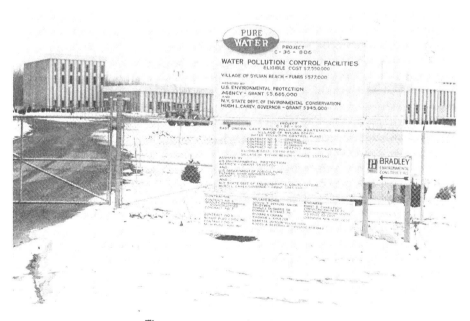

The new sewage treatment plant

URBAN RENEWAL — THE EDA GRANT
REBUILDS THE BEACH

The Amusement Mall — in the Midway

A play area for children — in the park

Weekly summer concerts at the Bandshell

Village Art Show — viewed through the bandshell's railing.

CROWDS, CROWDS, CROWDS

Fishermen line the canal on opening day

The Beach during a summer hot spell

Skeeballs roll in the Arcade

but problems remain

Bait people

Laughing people

(Photos/Rob Ziegler)

Loving people

Fishing people

Funny people

People at rest

People who remember

the experiences of several of Oneida's fairest at the blossoming resort of Fish Creek (Sylvan Beach). Gale's humor blooms in concert with the Beach.

Last Tuesday morning twenty young ladies, constituting aesthetic flowers of our village, might have been seen meandering towards the Midland Railroad Station with satchels, baskets, bandboxes and bundles, bound for that shrine of so many picnickers, Fish Creek.

On the arrival of the train they were soon aboard with many exclamations of fear least the car might break down with so many heavy weights, or the water tank run dry or the supply of peanuts give out. In due time they were landed at the bridge where they found a flotilla of Spencer's Venetian gondolas awaiting them under the command of Horace Baldwin, Terry Klock, and Willie Atherly.

They then descended to the boats and soon were reclining on the elegantly upholstered seats in picturesque attitudes and as they floated down the stream they formed a picture of perfect abandon of ease and grace that Raphael had he been alive would have given worlds to have conveyed on canvas. After a delightful ride through the winding creek, they reached the grounds and began to make pleasant acquaintance with flies, mosquitoes, bugs, snakes and other summer tourists of this fashionable resort.

Quite the clientele.

*   *   *   *   *

To say that Martin Cavana was ambitious is but an understatement. Ambition, as the bard relates, is made of "stern stuff" and Cavana had this quality. Born in Marcy Township, Oneida County, oldest of a family of thirteen, Martin Cavana exhibited his success drive early. When the Civil War broke out, Martin wanted to enlist as a Union drummer boy, but his age proved to be a handicap. He was too young, his family needed him, and all area military recruiters knew him. Martin's desire to serve the country, however, was so strong that he eventually yielded to it and boarded an Erie Canal barge in 1865, bound for New York City. There, he reasoned, he would be free to enlist and serve. When he arrived in the city he learned that Lee had surrendered to Grant at Appomatox. Cavana returned home, unsatisfied in his patriotism, but bursting with ambitious energy. This ardor would propel Cavana to become the hub of Sylvan Beach in the village's golden era.

* * * * *

Even in its best years, Sylvan Beach was not the resort mecca for all. It was a gay, carefree resort and, by manifesting this quality, it alienated certain groups. The black man's picnic caused many to snub their noses at the Beach. The *Camden Advance Journal* of July 16, 1896, reflected that attitude.

> The attraction at Sylvan Beach yesterday was the colored picnic. This vicinity contributed hundreds of white trash to the odoriferous gathering.

The *Advance Journal* of that time, a very straight paper, did not relish the good life of Sylvan Beach and put the village in a negative perspective whenever possible. The paper included articles about narrow escapes from allegedly dangerous carnival rides, incidents with inebriates, and the "ever-present" number of pick-pockets that slimed around the resort. It even wrote of indigestion caused by the resort's cuisine.

> One need not go dry at any beer fountain at Sylvan Beach on Sunday. All who apply simply

register, pay ten cents and are 'guests of the hotel.' A copper toed and iron bound sandwich and a glass of beer is set before them. The beer goes the way of all such stuff, but the sandwich is an everlasting article and does duty the entire season, unless someone with the digestion of an ostrich swallows it.

The *Advance Journal's* attitude was shared by many throughout history. Sylvan Beach was not a haven for the W.C.T.U. It never will be. Its fun-loving nature has given it life and prosperity. No Puritan could be happy here.

                    *   *   *   *   *

Railroads were Sylvan Beach's transportation lifeline in the Cavana years; they brought patrons en masse to the resort. In a lively correspondence, Gus Wemple of Boonville related to me his childhood impressions of those grand Beach trains. His thoughts further illustrate the spirit of excitement engendered by Cavana's Sylvan Beach.

> When very young, we all struggled to see who would be the first to see the whitecaps on the lake as the train backed into the long station track from the Y (the loop). Or who can forget the shrill whistle on the rear end of the train — now the head end — as the brakeman attached it to the air hose? There was some puzzlement in my mind the first time I saw a Lehigh Valley train backed up almost to the water on their side of Fish Creek. I wondered how it could jump the gap over the creek and get here — until the matter was quickly explained.

The Beach had its "Cave of the Winds," its "Trip Through Hell," its high divers and carnies galore, but not even the craftiest carnival man could conjure up a jumping train. But, oh, what an idea!

*   *   *   *   *

Russell's Hotel and Danceland, that mainstay of Sylvan Beach dancers in the 30's and 40's, was once called Hotel Nobles. William E. Russell purchased that old hotel and developed it into a class establishment, known for excellent food, lodging and the famous "taxi-dancing." The latter phenomenon, as you may recall, involved payment of a dime for the right to dance to a particular song. Russell's and the Pardee, Sennett and Quinn Dance Hall made taxi-dancing a big Beach attraction.

In its early years, Russell's did not employ the "Big Bands." Taxi-dancing music was provided by an assortment of local musicians, excellent tunesters in their own right. One of these groups was "Al Vogler's Midnight Serenaders," a spirited group of upstaters. As Vogler, Ken Lyons and company played their musical "sets" (three numbers), the dance floor rocked with body rhythm. The crowds loved tunes like "Whispering," "When Will the Sun Shine for Me," "Yes, We Have No Bananas" and the people went absolutely wild over the popular number, "Barney Google with the Goo-Goo-Googlie Eyes." Spicing up the show, Al and Ken would tour the room, sax and fiddle a-playing, bringing the sweet sounds close to their people. "These were the days," Al recalls with a smile, "The best days at the Beach. The band was everything. We enjoyed all of life's pleasures — girls adored the band members, Ma Russell treated us like kings, and musicians knew no prohibition. There was nothing like it — never has been."

And there probably never will be.

*   *   *   *   *

Throughout history, the Oneida Lake pike's succulent flesh has inspired fishermen, legally and otherwise, to invest hours in angling. The tasty fish has been served as prime table fare in Beach restaurants. Demand has often exceeded supply, however, and dining spots have turned to illegal sources, especially the Oneida Lake "fish pirate," to fill their pike quotas. The fish pirate was and is a daring character, a veritable man of the lake, knowledgable of the good fishing waters and adept in game warden elusion. In the 30's, the most renowned of these artful dodgers was the east shore's Jake Kyser. Operating out of South Bay, Kyser created a pirating legend in his time.

Kyser established his reputation in the late Cavana era. The target for constant game constable pursuit, he once boasted having five concurrent indictments for poaching. Never once, though, was he convicted. Harrassment and non-conviction bothered Jake, however, not so much for himself but for the people of the state. Once he wrote to a local paper arguing that New York's game constables and courts were wasting state funds. After all, he pointed out, court time is expensive and his numerous unproductive indictments did nothing but run up that expense. To Jake, the affairs were but a waste of money. This was some character.

And what a character he was. Once, on a bicycle, sporting a boxful of illegal pike, Jake met a game warden. The constable beckoned him to stop. Jake complied. The warden inquired as to the box's contents. Jake replied, "Warden, you wouldn't believe how full that box is — filled with pike." The warden laughed in disbelief and departed the scene. Jake laughed last.

Perhaps Jake Kyser's greatest triumph, however, was his mastery of lake navigation. Equipped with a small rowboat, Jake made many voyages into Oneida's tempests to rescue the capsized. No storm frightened him. No wave toppled his spirit. The lake was his lake, the fish his fish. Laws and societal limitations were not for Jake Kyser. He was a man of the lake. What a fortunate man.

*   *   *   *   *

The post World War II era at Sylvan Beach was, in contrast to much of the wartime, an era of relative prosperity. On one wartime July 4, for example, Emory Sauve grossed twenty-five cents on a normally prosperous shooting gallery game. The post-war brought far better times to the Beach. El Niles, former proprietor of Niles' Midway Lunch, remembers this time as "his best ever." The American economy, previously geared to military spending, was just adjusting to a more consumer-oriented era. "People couldn't buy much in stores," Niles recalls, "so they spent their money at the Beach. I sold hamburgs and hotdogs by the thousands."

An article in the Utica newspapers of this time echoed Niles' thoughts. The paper, under the title "Sylvan Beach Cleans Up for a Busy Summer Season," wrote:

> It's a wide place in the road. It's a place where they sell more neon signs than washing machines, more cotton candy than chocolate bars. It's a place where there are more cars than parking places, more people than beds. It's a place where 800 natives move over for 35,000 pleasure-bent city folk, for nine of the busiest, noisiest, most wondrous weeks of the season.

*   *   *   *   *

The Midway in the 50's Sylvan Beach was a varied place, with a spectrum of rides and games for the fun-loving crowd. Much of the success of the rides part of the 50's Midway was due to the labors of Francis and Iva Money and their sons, Ernest and Dean. The

Moneys' rides, which included the Octopus, Silver Streak, Caterpillar, Whip, and an original Parker Carousel, were top notch carnival entertainment. Success was synonymous with the Moneys' operation. Their recipe for attaining success was relatively simple. "We loved that business," says Iva Money, "and for us it was the only life. You've got to feel that way to succeed." In agreeing with his wife, Francis Money added, "We had an advantage over most others in the carnival trade. My sons and I were 'natural mechanics.' We did our own repairs. There were no outside labor costs."

Whatever their secret, the fact of the Moneys' once-booming operation remains. They and their talents helped make the 50's in Sylvan Beach into solid, profitable years. In addition to having prodigious business acumen, the Moneys were a warm, friendly people who delighted in sharing their lives and history with the interviewer. No writer could ask for more.

* * * * *

If I had a dollar for every carney, hotel keeper, barber, politician, poacher, merchant, or even Union Chapel board member whose name I omitted from my first edition, I would probably be a rich man. Like any community, Sylvan Beach has had thousands of persons grace its historical time lines. Many people have informed me, politely and otherwise (a humorous situation), of my personal omissions from edition one. I welcome such response, but find it difficult to convey to these people the point that the vast majority of those excluded were insignificant with regard to the total picture of Sylvan Beach history. Certainly these persons were considered important by their family and friends, but their impact on Sylvan Beach did not merit their inclusion. History is not a collection of scads and scads of trivia. History must be a story telling, analytical, yet interesting discipline. Filling pages with items like

Great Grandpa's popcorn machine and old Uncle Bill's bartending concoctions does not make for good history.

The list of names, of the people who were a part of the Beach's economic and social fibre, would fill pages on end. Among these people are carnival barkers like "Big Hearted" Leonard, Jack Patey of race-horse game fame; Bill Caguin, operator of the village's sole home-made ice cream business; Charles Owler, a gift shop entrepreneur; Goodrich and Steinburg, additional gift shop people; William McCarthy and his skating rink; William McCarthy, Jr., and his Elk Restaurant; William Rice, a meat man; Marge Doyle, founder of Marge's Sea Shell Inn; and James L. Bentley, a diversified businessman with interests in coal, construction, and soda pop.

Each of these persons is important in their own way. The list could go on and on. I wish that I could write about them. I can't. At least they can be mentioned.

*   *   *   *   *

Perhaps you recall Mabel Myers from my first edition. Mabel is the Fish Creek hamlet resident who dutifully tends to the landscaping-gardening chores at the Fish Creek Cemetery, site of the Spencer family plot. Fish Creek hamlet was the birthplace of Sylvan Beach, being the first home of the village's founding father, James D. Spencer. Mabel is James D.'s great-grand-daughter. She prides herself on her heritage and preserves much of it in a historical scrapbook.

Mabel Myers is an author. She has written a short survey history of Verona Beach which, sadly, is sequestered in the Verona town clerk's files. Mabel once made a stab at poetry, composing a verse entitled "Oneida Lake." Her words are warm and sincere, embracing the region she loves. In its simplicity, her poetry captures the emotions felt by many today and by countless thousands throughout history.

Oneida Lake

To live where one can see the waves,
  Caress the waters' edge
And watch a sailboat's gleaming mast,
  A seagull on a ledge.
How one can sit and dream away
  An idle, quiet hour
In fascination of a charm,
  Complete within its power.

The joy of living near a lake
  Is not a pleasure small.
Thats' why I'm ever grateful for
  A blessing not for all.
If ever from Oneida's shores
  It is for me to roam,
Returning, smell its cool, fresh air —
  I know that I am home.

And there's no place like it.

POSTLUDE

Something touched me deep inside,
The day the music died . . .

— Don McClean

From 1921 until 1977 Isaiah "Ike" Head and his wife, Minnie, operated "Head's Cash Store" at Sylvan Beach. The Heads were a wonderful couple whose warmth and friendship touched the lives of countless people. I was fortunate to be a member of that group. Knowing the Heads was a dear, invaluable experience. Their store was vintage Americana, an historian's delight. They encouraged me in my writing, eagerly responding to my many queries and increasing my Sylvan Beach historical files with veritable reams of data.

Isaiah and Minnie represented the best of Sylvan Beach. The village's history was their history; they took pride in it and enjoyed passing it on to others. Throughout Beach history they served their community. Minnie taught Sunday School and for years was an elementary teacher in the Sylvan-Verona Beach Common School. Ike was President of the Sylvan Beach Board of Trade in the 30's and 40's, a member of the Union Chapel Board for decades, Commander of the American Legion Post, and a strong supporter of community promotions. Ike's "Cash Store" gave credit; many Sylvan Beachers can thank him for their meals in hard times. Almost following Cavana's example, Ike Head helped to feed his people.

On a hot summer night in 1977, Ike and Minnie Head were robbed and beaten. Their assailants found little of value in the Head's home. Frustrated in larceny, they brutally assaulted the Heads.

In 1977 Ike Head was 83 years old. Minnie was 81. Normalcy never returned to their lives. Ike died in 1979. Minnie remains in the Oneida Hospital extended care facility.

It would be an easy matter to be bitter and hate-filled over this tragedy, but these are bad emotions that disgrace humankind. Rather, we must learn from Ike and Minnie's example. Sylvan Beach, if it is to prosper and fulfill its New Era goals, must place great value on the selfless community giving that was so much a part of the Heads' lives. Such giving produces a unanimity of purpose, so necessary for advancement. In this New Era the Beach has come far. Following the Heads' example, it can only go further.

In its religious origin, a postlude is a musical experience and this one is no exception. In 1974, Ike and Minnie introduced me to J. M. Filey's song, "Down at Sylvan Beach." Minnie often played this song on the family piano. The song captures a bit of the Cavana Era's spirit and a lot of the Heads' soul. Listen to the words:

On a bright summer's day, in all gladness we stray
Down the beach where joy is the rarest,
Meeting friends that are dear, we stroll on the pier
For a sail we will go with the fairest.

Oh the fishing is fine, the bathing sublime,
To Sylvan the crowds are all going
For it's a joy to be there, it excells everywhere
When cool welcome breezes are blowing.

Join, join, join the crowd down at Sylvan Beach,
Leave dull cares behind you, joy's within your reach
When you want to take your girl, and enjoy a
*   glorious whirl,*
There's no place in this wide, wide world
Like dear old Sylvan Beach.

On Oneida Lake's shore, with the girl you adore,
Her dear little hand you are squeezing,
And at night all the while
You can see the moon smile,
When this little girl starts her teasing.

For Sylvan I pine, its joys are divine,
There, nature is always entrancing,
And you start for a walk, sweet nothings you talk,
And what joy there is in the dancing!

At Sylvan Beach there has been much joy. I believe that it will continue. May all of you share in the dancing.

MY DEBTS

FOOTNOTES

CHAPTER ONE

[1] Indian language information taken from—
   a. Samuel W. Durant, *History of Oneida County*, Everts and Fariss, Philadelphia, 1878, in which the words were borrowed from Morgan's *League of the Ho-de-no-sau-nee.*
   b. E. B. O'Callaghan (ed.), *Documents Relative to the Colonial History of the State of New York*, Weed, Parsons and Company, Albany, 1861, V. III, p. 250.

[2] J. F. Stewart, *Souvenir Booklet of Sylvan Beach*, 1907, no pages numbered in the booklet.

[3] George W. Walter, *Chips and Shavings — Stories of Upstate New York*, Heritage Press, Sherburne, New York, 1966, pp. 86-87.

[4] W. L. Grant, *Voyages of Samuel DeChamplain, 1604 to 1618*, Charles Scribner's Sons, New York, 1907, p. 290.
   - and -
Clayton Mau, *The Development of Central and Western New York*, F. A. Owens Publishing Company, Dansville, New York, 1958, pp. 6-7.

[5] Alexander Flick (ed.), *History of the State of New York*, Columbia University Press, New York, 1933, v. I, p. 170-171.

[6] "Harmie" Roberts, *Scrapbook*, newspaper clippings from 1893 to 1899, from local (Rome and Oneida) papers.

[7] Francis Whiting Halsey, *The Old New York Frontier*, Charles Scribner's Sons, New York, 1901, p. 44.

[8] Hugh Hastings (ed.), *Ecclesiastical Records: State of New York*, James B. Lyon, Albany, 1901, v. II, p. 1392.

[9] *Ibid.*, p. 1380.

[10] Augustus Porter, *Narrative of the Early Years in the Life of Judge Augustus Porter*, Buffalo Historical Society, Buffalo, 1848, pp. 278-280.

[11] W. W. Canfield and J. E. Clark, *Things Worth Knowing About Oneida County*, Thomas J. Griffiths, Utica, 1909, p. 72.

[12] *Ibid.*, p. 73.

[13] John J. Vrooman, *Forts and Firesides of the Mohawk Country*, Baronet Litho Company, Johnstown, New York, 1951, p. 267.
   - and -
Archer Butler Hulbert, *Historic Highways of America*, The Arthur H. Clark Company, Cleveland, Ohio, 1903, p. 59.

[14] Vrooman, *op. cit.*, p. 269.

[15] *Ibid.*

[16] O'Callaghan, *op. cit.* v. V, p. 179.

[17] J. Elet Milton, "The Royal Blockhouse at the East End of Oneida Lake," 1961. All information in the following paragraph is borrowed from that paper.

[18] Francis Parkman, *The Conspiracy of Pontiac*, Little, Brown and Company, Boston, 1903.

[19] Milton W. Hamilton, *The Papers of Sir William Johnson*, The University of the State of New York, Albany, 1953.

[20] Rome Daily Sentinel, March 24, 1923.
[21] Quoted in Vrooman, *op. cit.*, p. 267.
[22] *Ibid.*, p. 269
[23] Gilbert Hagerty, *Massacre at Fort Bull*, Mowbray Company, Providence, Rhode Island, 1971, p. 79.
[24] Charles M. Snyder, *Oswego: From Buckskin to Bustles*, Ira J. Friedman Inc., Port Washington, New York, 1968, p. 12.
[25] Rome Daily Sentinel, March 24, 1923.
[26] Mau, *op. cit.*, p. 48.
[27] Jeptha R. Simms (ed.), *The Frontiersmen of New York*, George C. Riggs, Albany, 1883, v. II.
[28] *Ibid.*, p. 44.
[29] Quoted in Vrooman, *op. cit.*, p. 284
[30] O'Callaghan, *op. cit.*, v. X, p. 675.
[31] Elkanah Watson, *Men and Times of the Revolution*, Dana and Company, New York, 1856, p. 297.
[32] *Ibid.*, p. 341.
[33] Quoted in Harry F. Jackson, *Scholar in the Wilderness*, Syracuse University Press, Syracuse, 1963, p. 88.
[34] *Ibid.*, p. 91
[35] *Ibid.*
[36] *Ibid.*, p. 324.
[37] The following "Scriba Diary' 'is a histofictional account of major events in George Scriba's life. All facts originate from the *Scriba Papers*, New York State Library, State Education Building, Albany. The phrasing is mine, based on my reading of Scriba's personal papers. Granted, there is discrepancy between my writing style and that of my subject and the chronology is not as strict as some historians might want it, but this is historical fiction, designed to bring first-person narration and life to a normally analytical issue. The last diary entry is mostly Scriba's own pen, his words which explained his downfall.
[38] Duke De La Rochefaucault-Liancourt, *Travels Through the United States of North America, The Country of the Iroquois, and Upper Canada*, R. Phillips, London, v. I, pp. 347-348.
[39] Timothy Dwight, *Travels in New England and New York*, The Belknap Press of Harvard University Press, Cambridge, Massachusetts, 1969, v. IV, p. 88.
[40] *Ibid.*, p. 149.
[41] William W. Campbell (ed.), *The Life and Writings of DeWitt Clinton*, Baker and Scribner, New York, 1849, pp. 62-63.
[42] *Ibid.*, p. 64.
[43] The Milton Papers, Brewerton Library, Brewerton, New York.
[44] ...., *Centennial Address by John Seymour with Letters from Francis Adrian Van Der Kemp*, White and Floyd, Utica, 1877, pp. 100-101.
[45] Campbell, *op. cit.*, pp. 65-66.
[46] Quoted in Jackson, *op. cit.*, p. 95.
[47] Alexis de Tocqueville, *Memoirs, Letters and Remains*, Ticknor and Fields, Boston, 1862, v. I, p. 137.
[48] All quotes in this paragraph are from Liancourt, *op. cit.*
[49] J. H. French, *Historical and Statistical Gazeteer of New York State*, R. P. Smith, Syracuse, 1860, p. 521.
[50] T. Wood Clarke, *Emigres in the Wilderness*, MacMillan, New York, 1941, p. 36.
[51] Pomroy Jones, *Annals and Recollections of Oneida County*, Pomroy Jones, Rome, 1851, pp. 664-670.
[52] Ibid., p. 670.
[53] DeTocqueville, *op. cit.*, pp. 132-133.
[54] *Ibid.*, p. 134.

CHAPTER TWO

[1] Daniel E. Wager, *Our County and Its People*, The Boston Historical Company, Boston, 1896, p. 589.

[2] Pomroy Jones, *op. cit., p. 690*.

[3] *Ibid.*, pp. 694-695.

[4] Wager, *op. cit.*, p. 590

[5] Jones, *op. cit.*, pp. 695-696. The wolf hunt story comes from here.

[6] *Ibid.*, p. 662.

[7] Christian Schultz, *Travels on An Inland Voyage, 1807-1808*, Gregg Press, Ridgewood, New Jersey, 1968, p. 22.

[8] David Ellis *et al, A History of New York State*, Cornell University Press, Ithaca, 1967, p. 182.

[9] Thomas F. Gordon, *Gazetteer of the State of New York*, T. K. and P. B. Collins, Philadelphia, 1836, p. 566.

[10] Canal information taken from Noble E. Whitford, *History of the Canal System of the State of New York*, Brandow Printing, Albany, 1906, v. I & II, p. 1034.

[11] *Ibid.*

[12] Ulysses Prentiss Hedrick, *A History of Agriculture in the State of New York*, Albany, 1933, p. 250.

[13] Whitford, *op. cit.*

[14] *Ibid.*

[15] Schultz, *op. cit.*, p. 20.

[16] Durant, *op. cit.*, pp. 587-588.

[17] Wager, *op. cit.*, p. 89.

[18] *Ibid.*, p. 11.

[19] *Ibid.*

[20] Grantee-grantor Records, Oneida County, New York, County Office Building, Utica. The amount of land purchased by Spencer was totaled by the author, purchase by purchase.

[21] Wager, *op. cit.*, p. 89.

[22] Oneida County Records of Property Transactions, Book 339, p. 46.

[23] *Ibid.*

[24] Oneida Community Circular, May 19, 1873.

[25] Circular, December 9, 1872.

[26] Circular, December 23, 1872.

[27] *Souvenir — History and Attractions of Sylvan Beach*, Ryan and Burkhart, Oneida, around 1907.

[28] Wager, *op. cit.*, with arithmetic. Wager stated that Lyman Spencer operated the Forest Home for 17 years. Wager's book was copyrighted in 1896.

[29] Oneida County Grantee-grantor Records. The Spencer real estate sales were reviewed and counted for each year.

[30] Wager, *op. cit.*, p. 89.

[31] Rome Daily Sentinel, August 16, 1881.

[32] Rome Daily Sentinel, July 18, 1882.

[33] Cosmos' reply is based on Rome Daily Sentinel articles in the July 18, 1882, and August 15, 1882, issues.

[34] *The Algonquin*, a pamphlet sponsored by Stoddard and Garvin, published by the Oneida Dispatch, 1885 or 1886, p. 1.

[35] *Ibid.*, p. 3.

[36] *Ibid.*

[37] Rome Daily Sentinel, June 23, 1887.

[38] *Ibid.*

[39] Rome Daily Sentinel, May 16, 1886.

[40] Rome Daily Sentinel, May 8, 1886.

[41] From — an advertisement for the "Sylvan House,' taken from the Milton Papers.

[42] *Ibid.*

[43] Rome Daily Sentinel, July 3, 1886.

[44] Rome Daily Sentinel, August 19, 1886.

[45] Rome Daily Sentinel, July 31, 1889.

CHAPTER THREE

[1] Thomas Carlyle, *On Heroes and Hero Worship and the Heroic in History*, Chapman and Hall, London, 1840, p. 3.

[2] Cavana biographical information taken from —
　　a. Stewart, Souvenir Booklet, *op. cit.*
　　- and -
　　b. Syracuse Herald American, December 7, 1971.

[3] This begins a series of "news" clippings from a year in Sylvan Beach history. Most of the news blurps are fictitious, I have created them, basing all on historical facts. There was a Charles Bell, a Harmie Roberts, and obviously a Reuben Spencer. Local papers of that era ran a "Sylvan Beach social column." I have taken off on that theme, creating a year of news. The news talks of people with mumps, of the picnics, of fishing, of the weather, of life in Sylvan Beach, 1893.

For those of you who appreciate metaphor, my "running news" may prove provocative. That year, 1893, as I have written it, runs parallel to Sylvan Beach's fate in Cavana's time, beginning to end. At first there was budding growth, like that of Spring emerging from winter. Then the growth turned to full blossom as prosperity took its turn in Cavana's peak years. The blossom tapered and, with the death of Cavana in 1924, national calamity in the late '20's and a change in the Beach's basic resort nature it wilted in an era of resort turmoil.

[4] This date is generally agreed on by all sources at my disposal.

[5] Syracuse Herald, July 3, 1910.

[6] Oneida Dispatch, July 29, 1893.

[7] Rome Daily Sentinel, July 26, 1914.

[8] Article entitled the "Farmers Encampment," from the Roberts' scrapbook.

[9] Richard Stiller, *Queen of Populists: the Story of Mary Elizabeth Lease*, T. Y. Crowell Company, New York, 1970.

[10] Roberts' scrapbook, *op. cit.*

[11] *Ibid.*

[12] Oneida County Records of Property Transactions, Book 486, p. 62, and Book 499, p. 75.

[13] *New Century Atlas—Oneida County*, Century Map Company, Philadelphia, 1907, p. 157.

[14] Oneida County Records of Property Transactions, Book 553, p. 375.

[15] Rome Daily Sentinel, July 1, 1899.

[16] *Oneida Lake Homes: Summer Day Outing*, a pamphlet sponsored by the O. & W. Railroad, American Book Note Company, New York, 1903.

[17] Oneida County Records of Property Transactions, Book 563, p. 375.

[18] Utica Daily Press, September 18, 1914.

[19] Rome Daily Sentinel, September 18, 1914.

[20] From Sylvan Beach Official Stationary, about 1910.

[21] Stewart, *op. cit.*

[22] *Souvenir—History and Attractions of Sylvan Beach*, Ryan and Burkhart, Oneida, 1905-1907, Brewerton Library loan.

[23] Oneida Dispatch, May 3, 1960.

[24] Oneida County Records of Property Transactions, Book 599, pp. 105-108.

[25] From Sylvan Beach Stationary, about 1910.

26 This "tour" is another of my historical experiments. It is based on information gathered from numerous maps, pamphlets, and photographs from Sylvan Beach of Cavana's time. All of the material used in the tour is from work previously cited in this footnote section.
   I wish you a happy journey.
27 *Souvenir—History and Attractions, op. cit.*
28 Rome Daily Sentinel, November 4, 1903.
29 Utica Observer-Dispatch, July 1, 1907.
30 William F. Helmer, *O. & W.*, Howell-North, Berkely, California, 1959, p. 47.
31 *Ibid.,* p. 34.
32 Rochester Herald, August 12, 1910.
33 Helmer, *op. cit.*, pp. 205-206.
34 Syracuse Herald, October 27, 1901.
35 Syracuse Herald-Journal, February 21, 1907.
36 Syracuse Herald-Journal, March 25, 1908.
37 Syracuse Herald-Journal, August 4, 1909.
38 Rome Daily Sentinel, July 30, 1900.
39 Rome Daily Sentinel, July 26, 1919.
40 Syracuse Herald-Journal, August 4, 1909.
41 Milton Papers, Brewerton Library.
42 *Ibid.*
43 *Summer Day Outing: Oneida Lake Homes,* sponsored by the O. & W. Railroad, Wynkoop Hallenbeck Crawford Company, New York, 1898.
44 *Ibid.*
45 From the altar cornerstone, Union Church, Sylvan Beach.
46 Roberts' scrapbook, *op. cit.*, article entitled, "A Catholic Church to be Erected at this Resort."
47 Oneida Daily Dispatch, May 3, 1960. An article by Carl T. Moon is the basis for much of my de-incorporation story.
48 *Ibid.*
49 Oneida Daily Dispatch, August 5, 1910.
50 From a letter to Francis Hugo, Secretary of State, Albany, from Charles Wenzel, Oneida County Clerk, November 6, 1916.
51 Rome Daily Sentinel, January 8, 1912.
52 Mabel Myers, "Scrapbook," from a local paper, article dated January 6, 1939.

CHAPTER FOUR

1 Ellis, *op. cit.*, p. 563.
2 Rome Daily Sentinel, around 1917.
3 Helmer, *op. cit.*, p. 124.
4 *Ibid.*, p. 141.
5 Rome Daily Sentinel, August 14, 1933.
6 Rome Daily Sentinel, July 23, 1933.
7 Rome Daily Sentinel, July 5, 1935.
8 Rome Daily Sentinel, May 19, 1936.
9 Rome Daily Sentinel, July 7, 1934.
10 Rome Daily Sentinel, July 28, 1933.
11 Rome Daily Sentinel, August 18, 1933.
12 From the scrapbook of Hanna Sawner, a Rome Daily Sentinel article, dated November 6, 1937.
13 *Ibid.*
14 All dates which deal with Hotel Russell and its festivity come from Rome Daily Sentinel articles written during the hotel's heyday.

[15] *Sylvan Beach—The Playground of Central New York,* published by the Sylvan Beach Improvement Association, Malray Studios, Cazenovia, New York, 1955.

[16] Rome Daily Sentinel, July 17, 1933.

[17] Scrapbook, compiled unknown, property of Bernie Wameling, Sylvan Beach.

[18] Rome Daily Sentinel, July 13 and 14, 1933.

[19] Wameling scrapbook, *op. cit.*

[20] Phineas Camp, *Poems on the Mohawk Valley and On Scenes in Palestine,* Curtiss and White, Utica, 1859, pp. 88-91.

[21] Rome Daily Sentinel, July 18, 1939.

[22] Hanna Sawner scrapbook, *op. cit.*

[23] Rome Daily Sentinel, December 23, 1942.

[24] Rome Daily Sentinel, December 31, 1942.

[25] Rome Daily Sentinel, July 5, 1947.

[26] Russell dates from Rome Daily Sentinel, in the Russell's era.

[27] Rome Daily Sentinel, May 20, 1949.

[28] Rome Daily Sentinel, July 21, 1949.

[29] Rome Daily Sentinel, June 28, 1949.

[30] In the summer of 1972 I circulated a questionnaire in Sylvan Beach. These questionnaires were distributed at local businesses and by friends. I put about 200 in circulation and 50 were returned.

In the questionnaire I asked harmless questions such as number of years people had lived at the Beach, political preferences, and religion. These were but formalities. The gutsy questions concerned the economic climate of the Beach during the '50's and '60's.

Most of the town's businessmen replied to the questionnaire. Therefore, I consider it an accurate estimate of the Beach's fortunes during these years. Who would know better than the businessmen?

83% of those responding characterized the '50's as being prosperous times for the Beach. 60% characterized the '60's as being a depressed era for the town.

[31] Village Historian's scrapbook, Sylvan Beach.

[32] Mabel Myers' scrapbook, *op. cit.*

[33] Quotes, titles, etc., taken from three pamphlets, from the '50's, published by the Improvement Association. They are:

   a. *Sylvan Beach—The Playground of Central New York*

   b. (Visit Wonderful) *Sylvan Beach—The Playground of Central New York,* a longer, more detailed pamphlet.

   c. *Sylvan Beach, The Playground of Central New York,* the longest and most detailed of them all.

Color also distinguishes these three. The firs tis white, the second blue, and the third yellow.

[34] Utica Observer-Dispatch, May 19, 1957.

[35] Utica Observer-Dispatch, June 26, 1958, from a group of news clippings loaned to me by Gene Aubeuf, Sylvan Beach.

[36] *Ibid.*

[37] Oneida Daily Dispatch, August 25, 1959.

[38] Syracuse Herald-Journal, April 13, 1960.

[39] Myers' Scrapbook, *op. cit.*

[40] Phillip E. Greeson and George S. Meyers, *The Limnology of Oneida Lake: An Interim Report,* U.S. Department of the Interior Geological Survey in Cöoperation with the New York Conservation Department, 1969, p. 57.

[41] Quoted in the above, p. 16.

[42] Rome Daily Sentinel, July 16, 1960.

[43] Oneida Daily Dispatch, April 13, 1966.

[44] Incorporation and anti-incorporation data loaned to me by John DePerno and Eddie McCarthy, Sylvan Beach.

[45] Rome Sentinel, March 5, 1971.

BIBLIOGRAPHY

Anonymous, *Centennial Address by John Seymour with Letters from Francis Adrian Van Der Kemp*, White and Floyd, Utica, 1877.

Anonymous, *New Century Atlas—Oneida County*, Century Map Company, Philadelphia, 1907.

Camp, Phineas, *Poems of the Mohawk Valley and On Scenes in Palestine*, Curtiss and White, Utica, 1859.

Campbell, William W. (ed.), *The Life and Writings of DeWitt Clinton*, Baker and Scribner, New York, 1849.

Canfield, W. W., and Clark, J. E., *Things Worth Knowing About Oneida County*, Thomas J. Griffiths, Utica, 1909.

Carlyle, Thomas, *On Heroes and Hero Worship and the Heroic in History*, Chapman and Hall, London, 1840.

Clarke, T. Wood, *Emigres in the Wilderness*, MacMillan, New York, 1941.

Codman, Hislop, *The Mohawk*, Rinehart and Company, New York, 1948.

DeTocqueville, Alexis, *Memoirs, Letters and Remains*, Ticknor and Fields, Boston, 1862.

Disturnell, J., *The Picturesque Tourist: Being a Guide Through the State of New York,* J. Disturnell, New York, 1858.

Durant, Samuel W., *History of Oneida County*, Everts and Fariss, Philadelphia, 1878.

Dwight, Timothy, *Travels in New England and New York*, The Belknap Press of Harvard University Press, Cambridge, 1969.

Ellis, David, *et al, A History of New York State*, Cornell University Press, Ithaca, 1967.

Fairchild, Helen Lincklaen, *Francis Adrian Van Der Kemp*, G. P. Putnam's Sons, New York, 1903.

Flick, Alexander (ed.), *History of the State of New York*, Columbia University Press, New York, 1933.

French, J. H., *Historical and Statistical Gazetteer of New York State*, R. H. Smith, Syracuse, 1860.

Galpin, W. Freeman, *Central New York: An Inland Empire*, Lewis Historical Publishing Company, New York, 1941.

Gordon, Thomas F., *Gazetteer of the State of New York*, T. K. and P. G. Collins, Philadelphia, 1836.

Grant, W. L., *Voyages of Samuel De Champlain: 1604 to 1618*, Charles Scribners Sons, New York, 1907.

Hagerty, Gilbert, *Massacre at Fort Bull*, Mowbray Company, Providence, Rhode Island, 1971.

Halsey, Francis Whiting, *The Old New York Frontier*, Charles Scribner's Sons, New York, 1901.

Hamilton, Milton W. (ed.), *The Papers of Sir William Johnson*, The University of the State of New York, Albany, 1953.

Hastings, Hugh (ed.), *Ecclesiastical Records: State of New York*, James B. Lyon, Albany, 1901.

Hedrick, Ulysses Prentiss, *A History of Agriculture in the State of New York*, Albany, 1933.

Helmer, William F., *O. & W.*, Howell-North, Berkely, California, 1959.

Hulbert, Archer Butler, *Historic Highways of America*, The Arthur Clark Company, Cleveland, Ohio, 1903.

Jackson, Harry F., *Scholar in the Wilderness*, Syracuse University Press, Syracuse, 1963.

Jones, Pomroy, *Annals and Recollections of Oneida County*, Pomroy Jones, Rome, 1851.

Mau, Clayton, *The Development of Central and Western New York*, F. A. Owens Publishing Company, Dansville, New York, 1958.

O'Callaghan, E. B. (ed.), *Documents Relative to the Colonial History of the State of New York,* Weed, Parsons and Company, Albany, 1861.

Parkman, Francis, *The Conspiracy of Pontiac,* Little, Brown and Company, Boston, 1903.

Pierson, George Wilson, *Tocqueville and Beaumont in America,* Oxford University Press, New York, 1938.

Porter, Augustus, *Narrative of the Early Years in the Life of Judge Augustus Porter,* Buffalo Historical Society, Buffalo, 1848.

Rochefaucault-Liancourt, Duke De La, *Travels Through the United States of North America, The Country of the Iroquois, and Upper Canada,* R. Phillips, London, 1799.

Schultz, Christian, *Travels on an Inland Voyage, 1807-1808,* Gregg Press, Ridgewood, New Jersey, 1968.

Simms, Jeptha R. (ed.), *The Frontiersmen of New York,* George R. Riggs, Albany, 1883.

Snyder, Charles M., *Oswego: From Buckskin to Bustles,* Ira J. Friedman Inc., Port Washington, New York, 1968.

Stiller, Richard, *Queen of Populists: the Story of Mary Elizabeth Lease,* T. J. Crowell Company, New York, 1970.

Thwaites, Reuben Gold, *Early Western Travels: 1748 to 1846,* The Arthur H. Clark Company, Cleveland, 1906.

Vrooman, John J., *Forts and Firesides of the Mohawk Country,* Baronet Litho Company, Johnstown, New York, 1951.

Walter, George W., *Chips and Shavings—Stories of Upstate New York,* Heritage Press, Sherburne, New York, 1966.

Wager, Daniel E., *Our County and Its People,* The Boston Historical Company, Boston, 1896.

Watson, Elkanah, *Men and Times of the Revolution,* Dana and Company, New York, 1856.

Whitford, Noble E., *History of the Canal System of the State of New York,* Brandow Printing, Albany, 1906.

Wilson, Edmund, *Upstate,* Farrar, Strauss & Giroux, New York, 1971.

Newspaper Editions

Oneida Community Circular
May 19, 1873
December 9, 1872
December 23, 1872

Oneida Daily Dispatch
July 29, 1893
August 5, 1910
August 25, 1959
May 3, 1960
April 13, 1966

Rochester Herald
August 12, 1910

Syracuse Herald
October 27, 1901
July 3, 1910

Syracuse Herald-American
December 7, 1971

Syracuse Herald-Journal
February 21, 1907
March 25, 1908

August 4, 1909
April 13, 1960

Syracuse Post-Standard
January 8, 1912

Utica Observer-Dispatch
July 1, 1907
May 19, 1957
June 26, 1958
August 9, 1970

Utica Daily Press
September 18, 1914

Rome Daily Sentinel
July 19, 1881
August 16, 1881
July 18, 1882
May 8, 1886
May 15, 1886
July 3, 1886
August 19, 1886
July 23, 1887

July 31, 1889
July 1, 1889
July 30, 1900
November 4, 1903
January 8, 1912
July 26, 1919
March 14, 1923
July 13, 1933
July 14, 1933
July 17, 1933
July 23, 1933
July 28, 1933
August 14, 1933
August 18, 1933
July 7, 1934
July 5, 1935
May 19, 1936
November 6, 1937
July 18, 1939
May 20, 1949
June 28, 1949
July 5, 1951
July 16, 1960
March 5, 1971

Oneida County Records of Property Transactions

1. All Spencer family purchases, 1850 to 1880.
2. All Spencer family sales, 1872 to 1891.
   These are found in grantee-grantor books under Spencer, James D. and Reuben J.

3. *Individual Transactions*

Book	*Page*	*Book*	*Page*
339	46	499	75
434	245	553	375
486	62	599	105 to 108

Endpapers' Lake Oneida Map

The use of this map was granted the author by The Anglers' Association of Onondaga, a non-profit conservationist group that has enriched Lake Oneida's environment since 1890. These maps are a primary means of funding for the Association and may be purchased in most Lake Oneida area bait and tackle stores. They are not sold by the author.

Papers, Pamphlets and Reports

Anonymous, *Souvenir—History and Attractions of Sylvan Beach*, Ryan and Burkhart, Oneida, around 1907.
Anonymous, *Oneida Lake Homes: Summer Day Outing*, sponsored by the O. & W., Railroad, American Bank Note Company, New York, 1903.
Anonymous, *Summer Day Outing: Oneida Lake Homes*, sponsored by the O. & W. Railroad, Wynkoop Hallenbeck Crawford Company, New York, 1898.
Anonymous, *Sylvan Beach—The Playground of Central New York*, published by the Sylvan Beach Improvement Association, a series of three pamphlets from the 1950's.
Anonymous, *The Algonquin*, sponsored by Stoddard and Garvin of Oneida, the hotel's owners, published by the Oneida Dispatch, 1886-1886.
Greeson, Phillip E., and Meyers, George S., *The Limnology of Oneida Lake: An Interim Report*, U.S. Department of the Interior Geological Survey in Cooperation with the New York State Conservation Department, 1969.
Milton, J. Elet, various papers, records, books collected at the Brewerton Library, Brewerton, New York.
Stewart, J. F., *Souvenir Booklet of Sylvan Beach*, 1907.
Also—1. Martin Cavana's Sylvan Beach stationery
2. The Francis Hugo Letter, November 6, 1916
3. Sylvan Beach Incorporation Data, loaned by Ed McCarthy and John DePerno

Scrapbooks

Cleveland, Henrietta, and Sadowski, Francis, "Sylvan Beach Historians Scrapbook," being a collection of articles from local papers and miscellaneous pamphlets, postcards, etc., begun since the village's recent incorporation.
Gahan, Richard, "Railroad and Steamboat Scrapbook," being a collection of articles about the South Bay Railroad Company, the Sagamore steamboat, etc.
Head, Isaiah, "Harmie Roberts Scrapbook," Sylvan Beach in the 1890's.
Myers, Mabel, "personal Scrapbook," being a collection of Beach news clippings dating back through the 1940's.
Sawner, Lillian, "Hanna Sawner Scrapbook," being a collection of Sylvan Beach social trivia, 1920-1960.
Wameling, Bernie, "Ice Scrapbook," being the telltale account of the effects of ice storms and early freezes on Sylvan Beach, Oneida Lake and the Barge Canal. Illustrated and very animated.

— PERSONALS —

These people helped me create this history. In doing so, they not only assisted the book's growth, but became a beautiful part of the work themselves. I give them now, my friends and acquaintances, my hearty thanks.

There are many people who will be omitted from this list, simply because I never bothered to learn their names. To these people, the "unnamed majority," I send apologies and gratitude. Most were Oneida "lake people." Just seeing them or chatting for the passing moment, even just being around them made my work easier and purposeful. They deserve to have their history written.

Mary Adams
Eleanor Armstrong
Gene Aubeuf
Howard Beneke
Nat Boxer
Glenn Chesebrough
Warren Clemens
John Clements
Henrietta Cleveland
Francis Coleman
John DePerno
Bill Donlon
David Ellis
Bill Ennis
Dick Gahan
Bob Grube

David Goff, Ann White, the
    Madison County
    Historical Society
Isaiah and Minnie Head
Jane
Linda Krueger
Gary Kulik
Moe LaBella
Art Mengel
Ruth Metz
Chester Mazerowski, No Hope
    and Little Hope
Ed McCarthy
David Millar
Mabel Myers
The Oneida County
    Historical Society

Maurice Peck
Paul and Joyce Pratt
Henry and Fran Sadowski
George and Lil Sawner
Scotty
Victor Serby
Margaret McAndrew Spellicy
Eddie Stewart, Sr.
Eddie Stewart, Jr.
Dick Sullivan
Cornelius Van Der Linde
Bernie Wameling
Don Wells
Bobbie Williams
Harry Williams
Rob Zeigler

Now small fowls flew screaming over the yet yearning gulf. A sudden surf beat against its steep sides, then all collapsed, and the great shroud of the sea rolled on as it did ten thousand years ago.

—*Herman Melville*

SYLVAN BEACH, NEW YORK — A HISTORY strives to avoid the trivia tradition of most local history and works to capture the essences, "moving forces" if you will, within the several eras experienced by that village. In this book you will find poetry, the short story, histofictional tours, purposeful photographs as well as "straight," analytical history. It is the author's ambition that the combination of these expository elements will give you the best possible, most enjoyable history of Sylvan Beach.

(Photo/Nat Boxer)

Jack Henke received his B.A. degree in history from Hamilton College in 1972 and his M.A.T. degree in the same field from Brown University in 1973. In addition to his Sylvan Beach writing, he has authored *Lawyers and the Law in New York*, a centennial book from the New York State Bar Association. His articles have appeared in *The History of Oneida County* and *The Hamilton Alumni Review*. He has lectured at numerous historical forums throughout upstate New York. Currently, he is a teacher at Brookfield Central School and, in the summer, spends many an enjoyable hour on the waters of Oneida.

Rear Cover —
An advertisement from Russell's Hotel and Danceland, the Sylvan Beach home to America's "Big Bands."